James Morton

Southern Plants for Southern Homes

Southern Floriculture

James Morton

Southern Plants for Southern Homes
Southern Floriculture

ISBN/EAN: 9783741197703

Manufactured in Europe, USA, Canada, Australia, Japa

Cover: Foto ©Thomas Meinert / pixelio.de

Manufactured and distributed by brebook publishing software
(www.brebook.com)

James Morton

Southern Plants for Southern Homes

Southern Floriculture,

BY JAMES MORTON.

Price, handsomely bound in cloth, gold embossed, $1.00; paper, 60c. Mailed free on receipt of price.

" Southern Floriculture " will teach you how to grow these flowers.

We have found a great need for this work, and take pleasure in offering it to our friends and patrons. It is respectfully dedicated to the flower-loving ladies of the South. It is devoted to the culture and propagation of all of the most popular flowering and ornamental plants of the present day, with hints on their origin and introduction. It treats on all the diseases, with remedy, the different classes of plants are subject to, and gives varieties best adapted to the climate and soil of the South. It exposes the humbugs of Horticulture, and is truly a Southern book that every flower-loving lady in the South should read. The chapter on the propagation of the Rose is alone worth the price of the book It is written in a pleasing style, and will not only prove instructive, but interesting, to all parties interested in Floriculture.

Owing to a rush in the publishing house, the book will not be complete before the first week of March, at which time it will be sent to all who wish it We also take this opportunity to thank the numerous friends who have already sent their names for a copy, and ask their kind indulgence until the time before mentioned.

We want a reliable lady agent in every city in the South to act as agent for this book. Good commission. Address, J. MORTON, Clarksville, Tenn.

Our Spring Flower Display.

So great was the success of our Fall display of Chrysanthemums that at the request of a number of our friends and patrons we have determined to give a Spring Flower Show, the particulars of which we regret we cannot give now, as our arrangements for this display are at present incomplete. All friends interested will, however, be supplied later with full information upon enquiry. About the first week of February, and lasting for a period of three or four weeks, we will have in full bloom in our greenhouses several thousand Hyacinths, together with hundreds of Azalias, Primroses, Freezias, Fuchsias, Lilies, Bouvardias, Roses, Astibile, Camellias, Orchids and an innumerable lot of beautiful flowers that come invariably at that season ; they will all be arranged in our larger exhibition greenhouse, interspersed with fine Palms, Ferns and richly-colored foliage plants, and we contemplate a display of unsurpassing beauty, and herewith cordially extend an invitation to all our friends to come and see us at about that time. Parties intending to come from a distance had better write in advance, so we can more accurately name the time when the flowers will be at their prettiest and can be seen to the best advantage.

W. P. Titus, Printer and Binder, Clarksville, Tenn.

INTRODUCTORY.

A S the season for gardening operations is again at hand, and the busy housewife will soon have to determine what is best to plant in the domestic flower plot to give beauty to the family abode, fragrance to the surroundings, and a high standard of refinement to the entire home circle. To assist in the deliberations of many thousands of fair florist now planning for their Spring task in Floriculture, we take much pleasure in presenting our Catalogue for the Spring of 1899, and trust it may prove of some interest to you. The ever increasing demand for the unexcelled collection of plants we offer in it, is the best criterion that our patrons appreciate our efforts to do a square, honest business. We enumerate nothing but what is good, and quote them at prices so reasonable that all may buy. We have endeavored to offer only the very best in the different classes of plants, so that our customers will not be confused in looking over long lists of varieties that differ little except in name. Our Roses and Chrysanthemums cannot be excelled. We find a wonderful increase in the demand for large Roses, and to meet this growing demand we have a large assortment of all the most popular varieties of large size. Our collection of Chrysanthemums is unquestionably the finest on this continent. All the newest and oldest of great merit are to be found in our collection, gathered from innumerable sources to make one grand collection unrivalled in America or elsewhere. During our show last November, hundreds of people visited our display daily for a period of about three weeks, and so loud was the praise and excitement so great, that special trains were run to Clarksville from several points with excursion parties to see them, and the L. & N. Railroad kindly gave a reduced rate to our place on all their regular trains in order

that every flower loving friend from far and near might have an opportunity to behold the great beauty of the "Queen of Autumn." We touch "Novelties" but slightly, as there is more opportunity to be humbugged by investing in them than anything we know of. The many novelties offered are in some cases a lot of old renamed, discarded stuff, given some high sounding name and scattered broadcast over the land, only to hear each purchaser say after a year's cultivation of it, "sold again." There is enough of good well known varieties in every class of plants beautiful enough to give all the enjoyment to be found in their particular class, to a majority of plant buyers. We guarantee

"Aint They Pretty."

satisfaction in every case, and if we have a dissatisfied customer, it is because we do not know it. Our business last season increased fifty per cent. over the previous year, and the outlook for this season is now encouraging. We have the finest stock of plants to select from that it is possible to accumulate. We would bo pleased where convenient if our customers could pay us a visit and see our greenhouses and flowers. We have, owing to our large shipments over the lines of the Southern Express Company, secured a special rate of 25 per cent. less than their regular charges. The many flattering letters received by us would fill a book as large as this Catalogue, all of which we are most grateful for, and considered by us a high compliment to our business methods, and we here wish to return to all our heartfelt thanks for the words of encouragement as well as for the liberal patronage given us, and it is almost needless to add that it shall be our aim in the future as well as in the past to endeavor to please each one of our customers. The Southern people can never have a large and enterprising floral establishment if by their joint co-operation they do not help to make it so. It is needless to send to Northern florists for what you cau secure nearer home. Apart from this, however, we would be slow to solicit a single order from any individual whatever upon the grounds that it is our good fortune to live in the Sunny South. It is only because we can do as well for you and in most cases better, that we ask for a share of your patronage. With kind wishes for a happy New Year to all our customers and friends,

We remain, most truly,   JAMES MORTON, Manager.

J. J. CRUSMAN, Proprietor.

A FEW POINTS—READ BEFORE ORDERING.

OUR TERMS.
Our terms are invariably Cash with the order.

ORDERS.
Remember all orders, large or small, are shipped in the order they are received.

VISITORS WELCOME.
Visitors are always welcome, as we have something of interest for them to see at all seasons of the year.

EXPRESS.
All orders for goods not stating the mode of transportation will be sent by express at the purchaser's expense.

SEEDS.
We have gone entirely out of the Seed business, and will in future devote our attention to the growth of plants exclusively.

IN REMITTING,
send Money Order or Draft: if in currency, invariably register the letter, as we will not be responsible for remittances otherwise made.

PLEASE USE THE ENCLOSED ORDER SHEET.
If you have other matter to write, use separate paper or the opposite side of the sheet, but do not mix the order up with other matter.

PACKING BY MAIL.
We use a strong wooden box to pack in. Plants are all laid one way and securely fastened, thereby avoiding any crushing or mangling of leaves.

POSTAGE STAMPS.
When you cannot procure a Money Order and cannot make change otherwise we will accept Postage Stamps. We would prefer 2, 5 and 10-cent stamps.

OUR AIM.
Our desire is to deal with our customers, that they may continue to favor us with their orders in the future, and they may rely on our endeavors to give satisfaction in every instance.

POSTAL NOTES
are very convenient for small amounts, but are no more safe than money sent in an ordinary letter, as they cannot be duplicated if lost, and anybody that gets them can collect them.

HYACINTHS, TULIPS AND FALL BULBS.
We will issue about September 1st, a Catalogue of Bulbs and Winter flowering plants, which will be mailed to all of our customers who have ordered of us during the last year. Others who wish it are requested to write for it.

OUR SHIPPING FACILITIES.
Our shipping facilities are first-class, and the rates by express or freight from this point are much less to all the States South of us than they are from any of the Eastern floral establishments; the time occupied in transit is also much less.

HAVE YOUR GOODS SENT BY EXPRESS,
if possible, is always our advice, as you invariably get your plants in better condition; and, as an inducement, we send a lot of plants extra to help pay express charges, and we feel ourselves repaid by the better satisfaction our shipments will give you.

ORDERS FOR LESS THAN ONE DOLLAR
will not be filled unless fifteen cents additional to the price of the plants to be sent to pay postage. It is quite as much trouble to handle, and requires nearly as much postage to mail, a fifty cent order as it does one for two or three dollars' worth of plants.

COLLECTIONS.
Parties having no knowledge of the different habits and adaptability of plants will do well to write and give us the particulars of the kind of beds they wish them for, or if for window culture, we can select them in most all cases to give the best satisfaction desired.

WHEN OUR LIABILITY FOR LOSS CEASES,
We take a receipt for all plants delivered in good order to carrying company, when our liability ceases, and the plants are at the risk of parties ordering. We make no charge for drayage or packing. If mistakes occur, notify us at once; otherwise, we are not responsible.

LETTERS AND PACKAGES.
Letters travel somewhat faster in mails than packages, so, if we write you a letter, and it reaches you before the plants, wait a day or two before writing. and give them the necessary time, and in ninety-nine cases in every hundred all will came out right, saving both of us the trouble of writing.

BE PATIENT.
In our busy season the office work is so pressing that packages of plants frequently leave the greenhouse before we get an opportunity to write, and as this is unavoidable, we beg our customers, if any plants are missing, to kindly wait two or three days for a letter of explanation before informing us of the shortage.

OUR LOW PRICES.
A careful comparison of our prices with those of other growers will show that we offer plants much cheaper than the same grade of stock can be purchased for at any other establishment in the country. In proof of this we are willing to duplicate the prices of any first-class and reliable house in the United States on plants, in this Catalogue.

O. O. D. ORDERS.

C. O. D. orders must be accompanied by at least one-fourth of the amount in cash, and the parties ordering are to pay the express charges for collecting. Large orders of shrubbery, trees, etc., can go by ordinary freight, by consigning to our own order and sending bill of lading by express, C. O. D., endorsed to parties ordering. Heavy express charges are thus avoided and collections facilitated.

OUR PLANTS.

Plants offered in this Catalogue are none of your puny, weak little things that take till Fall to see what you get; but are grown in pots ranging in size from $2\frac{1}{2}$ to 4 inches, according to varieties of plants. We need not mention this to old customers who know what kind of plants we send out, but this Catalogue will be received by many people who never saw our plants or received our Catalogue before. Patrons can always depend on getting their money's worth, and more, too, as we are very liberal with our extras.

MISTAKES.

If anything is wrong with your order, do not think we intended it, for we have no interest in so doing; out interest is to give satisfaction, and that we are determined to do; so should an error occur, kindly put it down as a mistake, notify us, and we will put it right. We wish our customers would, in every case, keep a copy of their order, and verify it on arrival of plants; this will prevent mistakes as to what they "thought" they ordered, but which was never written upon their order sheet; and if not too much trouble, please drop us a card on the arrival of the goods. We are glad to know when you are pleased, and we wish to know of any dissatisfaction, that we may make it right.

PLEASE BE CAREFUL

and write your Name and Address plainly. We can readily make out what is wanted in an order, as we are acquainted with the names of all our plants, but we have no means of knowing what your name is or how it should be spelled unless you write it plainly. We receive many orders that are well written throughout, but when we look to see who sends them, the name is so carelessly written that we are obliged to guess at it. Indeed, some forget entirely to sign their name. Again we would say, Please Sign your Name Carefully, as it will save us much annoyance, and possibly, prevent errors.

BULBS GIVEN AWAY!

Ten Handsome Presents to be Distributed
in September.

AS an inducement to ladies to get up clubs, we have decided to offer as premiums a choice assortment of Spring and Winter flowering bulbs in ten separate collections, to be selected from our Fall Catalogue as soon as it is issued in September. The bulbs will all be of the finest quality, and will consist chiefly of Hyacinths, Tulips, Crocus, Narcissus, Lilies, Iris, Crown Imperials, and other popular flowering bulbs to the amount of

FIFTY DOLLARS.

These presents are altogether an outside matter, and will have nothing to do with the other inducements offered elsewhere to originators of clubs. The parties that will secure the above presents will be notified by letter from us in May, when our shipping season closes, and their name published in our Fall Catalogue and their presents sent prepaid to them in September.

We offered this inducement for the first time last Spring with good results. The names of the successful parties was published in our Fall Catalogue, and the bulbs sent to them as we promised. We will mail a Fall Catalogue to any one who may desire it.

The bulbs will be distributed to the successful ladies or others as follows :
For the originator of the largest club, $20.00 in bulbs.
For the originator of the 2d largest club, $12.00 in bulbs.
For the originator of the 3d largest club, $5.00 in bulbs.
For the originator of the 4th largest club, $4.00 in bulbs.
For the originator of the 5th largest club, $3.00 in bulbs.
For the originator of the 6th largest club, $2.00 in bulbs.
For the originator of the 7th largest club, $1.00 in bulbs.
For the originator of the 8th largest club, $1.00 in bulbs.
For the originator of the 9th largest club, $1.00 in bulbs.
For the originator of the 10th largest club, $1.00 in bulbs.

INDUCEMENTS TO CLUBS.

Although prices are low in this Catalogue for all classes of plants, most liberal terms are offered to friends who are inclined to obtain orders from others, and to secure thereby some fine specimens free of cost for themselves. In making up a club order it is important to state the sum sent by each member and the plants wanted, that they may be separately packed and confusion avoided when the plants are distributed. The full address of each is required. The following are the rates from $3.00 to $20.00 (larger sums in proportion):

For a $3.00 club order the originator may select in plants 50 cents.
For a $4.00 club order the originator may select in plants 75 cents.
For a $5.00 club order the originator may select in plants $1.00.
For a $6.00 club order the originator may select in plants $1.10.
For a $7.00 club order the originator may select in plants $1.25.
For a $8.00 club order the originator may select in plants $1.50.
For a $9.00 club order the originator may select in plants $1.75.
For a $10.00 club order the originator may select in plants $2.00.
For a $15.00 club order the originator may select in plants $3.00.
For a $20.00 club order the originator may select in plants $4.00.
For a $25.00 club order the originator may select in plants $5.00

CHEAP LIST.

THE following collections, to be sent by express only, are very desirable to those who want a nice flower bed and care nothing about having the names put on the each plant, the doing of which during the busy season consumes valuable time. We desire it distinctly understood that the plants in these collections are just as good and desirable in every way, and probably would be better than the individually selected plants at more than double the price.

ONE DOLLAR COLLECTIONS.

Owing to a large increase in our facilities for raising plants this last Summer, we are able to offer plants in the following collections at the exceedingly low rate of 25 plants for $1.00, by express only, and no premiums with these collections. If wanted by mail, add 15 cents extra:

25 Hollyhocks.	25 Violets.	25 Nasturtiums.
25 Verbenas.	25 Heliotropes.	25 Ageratums.
25 Colens.	25 Tuberoses.	25 Salvias.
25 Pansys.	25 Gladiolus.	25 Cannas.
25 Geraniums.	25 Centaurea.	25 Sweet Allysums.
25 Achyranthus.	25 Chrysanthemums.	25 Mahernia.
25 Carnations.	25 Asters.	25 Tulips.

If the parties ordering prefer, they may select 5 plants from 5 of the different collections; thus, 5 Geraniums, 5 Pansys, 5 Tuberoses, 5 Chrysanthemums and

5 Verbenas. Not less than 5 plants from any one collection to make up the 25 as offered for $1.00. The plants will be packed nicely in a small basket, and sent by express. Six collections for $5.00.

COLLECTION OF PLANTS FOR FIVE DOLLARS.

BY EXPRESS ONLY.

The following collection, containing one hundred and fifty-six plants for $5.00, is the cheapest ever offered, and every one of them are fine strong plants that will grow rapidly and make beautiful any home and its surroundings for the Summer. and many of them will stand the Winter and come again the following season. Nobody should neglect to beautify the surroundings of their home with an offer like this before them. The selection of all the varieties must be left with us. We cannot hunt up named varieties at this price. They will all be packed carefully in a light box or basket, and sent anywhere by express for $5.00. One-half the collection for $3.00. No premium with this collection:

6 Everblooming Roses.	6 Pansys.	4 Violets.
6 Chrysanthemums.	6 English Daisys.	4 Rose Geraniums.
6 Achyranthus.	6 Paris Daisys.	4 Lantanas.
6 Fuchsias, named.	6 Verbenas.	4 Abutilons.
6 Geraniums.	6 Asters.	4 Sweet Allysum.
6 Tuberoses.	6 Ageratums.	2 Evening Glorys.
6 Carnations.	6 Coleus.	2 Plumbagos.
6 Heliotropes.	4 Night-Blooming Jasmine.	2 Hibiscus.
6 Gladiolus.	4 Feverfews.	2 Dahlias.
6 Begonias.	4 Hollyhocks.	2 Callas.
6 Salvius.	4 Mahernia.	2 Lautanas.

MIXED DOLLAR COLLECTIONS.

BY EXPRESS ONLY.

CHEAPNESS and merit being considered, it will be seen that where persons are not well acquainted with different varieties, so as to enable them to make judicious selections, these sets offer great advantages, and parties will usually get as good selections as they could make themselves, our aim being as far as possible to satisfy every customer that favors us with an order. The choice of varieties in these sets must be left entirely to us, as we positively cannot afford, at the collection prices, to permit customers to name the plants. These collections are subject to the following conditions: That persons ordering are only to name the letter or numbers, designating the collection or collections wanted, as it takes too much valuable time to read long letters, giving detailed lists of plants in each collection desired. Simply the letter of the collection is all sufficient. Entirely our selection of varieties. All labeled. These collections are not entitled to premiums. Parties ordering from this list will order by letter. ☞Give this mode of purchasing plants a trial. We are confident it will please you. No premiums with these collections. Parties ordering from this list will order by letter:

A—25 Alternantheas, of sorts.
B—25 Geraniums, double and single, all kinds.
C—25 Verbenas, all sorts; makes a fine bed.
D—25 Begonias, flowering varieties.
J—25 Basket and Vase Plants, in variety.
K—25 Fuchsias, double and single.
L—25 Chrysanthemums; Japanese and Pompon.
M—25 Roses, Geraniums, Coleus and Achranthus.
N—25 Geraniums, Verbenas, Coleus and Heliotropes.
O—25 Coleus, Heliotropes, Ageratums, Lantanas and Feverfews.
P—25 Carnations, Geraniums, Fuchsias, Begonias and Coleus.
Q—25 Petunias, Verbenas, Heliotropes, Lantanas and Feverfews.

E—25 Heliotropes, different shades.
F—25 Coleus; makes a beautiful foliago bed.
G—25 Salvias, numerous kinds.
H—25 Ageratums, an assortment.
I—25 Carnations, splendid kinds.
R—25 Roses, Geraniums and Verbenas.
S—25 Abutilous, Carnations, Coleus, Ageratums and Verbenas.
T—25 Carnations, Chrysanthemums, Achranthus, Ageratums and Coleus.
U—25 Miscellaneous Plants, all kinds.
V—25 Tuberoses, Gladiolas, Cannas and Calladiums.
W—25 Geraniums, Tuberose, Gladiolas and Pansies.
X—25 Pansies, Heliotropes, Geraniums and Lantanas.

ONE DOLLAR MAIL COLLECTIONS.

OOK carefully at this offer for one dollar. There are many bright and happy homes throughout the South where intelligence is supreme and consequently good flowers appreciated, that are not fortunate to have an express office convenient to them. To place our flowers within the reach of such people, we have prepared the following collections that we will send free, postpaid, through the mail, for one dollar, packed carefully in a nice wooden box. Any one of these collections will make a handsome bed, and nothing helps to make a home more cheerful than a neat flower garden, however small. If preferred, parties may select four plants from any five collections, and make up their twenty plants in that way. Any three collections for 2.50, or six for 5.00.

20 Geraniums.	20 Gladiolus.	20 Hellotropes.
20 Chrysanthemums.	20 Verbenas.	20 Coleus.
20 Carnations.	20 Asters.	20 Achyranus.
20 Tuberoses.	20 Fuchsias.	20 Violets
20 Pansys.	20 Salvias.	

MIXED MAIL COLLECTIONS FOR ONE DOLLAR.

PLEASE ORDER BY NUMBER.

1—4 Geraniums, 4 Roses, 3 Coleus, 3 Heliotrope, 3 Pansys, 3 Verbenas.

2—4 Fuchsias, 4 Carnations, 4 Salvia, 3 Tuberoses, 3 Gladiolus, 2 Plumbagos.

3—6 Violets, 6 Daisys, 4 Pansys, 2 Abutilons, 2 Hollyhocks.

4—4 Lantanas, 4 Petunias, 2 C. Myrtle, 3 Begonias, 3 Chrysanthemums, 4 Smilax.

5—4 Roses, 4 Carnations, 4 Hollyhocks, 3 Scented Geraniums, 3 Tuberoses.

6—6 Cardations, 6 Pansys, 6 Asters, 1 Calla, 1 Lily of the Valley.

7—6 Chrysanthemums, 2 Violets, 2 Roses, 2 Abutilons, 2 Salvias, 6 Fuchsias.

8—2 Crape Myrtle, 2 Feverfew, 4 Roses, 4 Hollyhocks, 6 Garden Pinks, 2 Violets.

There is not a home in the South or a person that receives this Catalogue, but what can use at least one of these collections to advantage. If you are boarding at a hotel and have no place to put them out, they will make a nice present for a friend not so situated, and will afford pleasure and remembrance all the Summer long. We ask therefore as an acknowledgement that this Catalogue is appreciated, an order for at least one dollar's worth of flowers, so that your name may go permanently on our books as customers, and continue to receive our Catalogues.

BY MAIL OR EXPRESS FOR ONE DOLLAR.

14 Roses.
14 Hardy flowering plants.
8 Evening Glorys or Moon flowers.
10 Bouvardias.

14 Begonias.
12 Calla lilies.
10 Mixed evergreens and hardy flowering shrubs.
12 Succulent plants, Sedum,

Echeveria, Catus, &c.
14 Mixed Abutilons and Lantanas.
16 Roses.

Five Lantanas, five Dusty Miller, twelve Coleus and one Abutilon. This makes a nice bed with Abutilon in center, Lantanas next, Dusty Miller next, and Coleus on the outside.

One Azalea, one Camelia and two Dracenas. The last two collections by Express only.

OUR REFERENCE.

This edition of our Catalogue will reach many who have never purchased of us before, and to assure them they are dealing with responsible parties we give below some reference as to our standing:

Dunn or Bradstreet's Commercial Report.
Semidt & Zeigler, New Orleans.
Thurber, Wyland & Co., New York.
Porter & Maerae, Memphis.
American Nat. Bank, Nashville.
Farmers & Mer. Nat. Bank, Clarksville.
Clarksville, Nat. Bank, Clarksville.

Smith Bros., New Orleans.
Sawyer, Wallace & Co., N. York.
E. C. Hazard & Co., New York.
Oliver Finnie & Co., Memphis.
First Nat. Bank, Clarksville.
Franklin Bank, "
Northern Bank, "

THE QUEEN OF FLOWERS,

ROSE is the "Queen of Flowers." No garden, however small, is complete without Roses. There are no flowers grown that are more universally admired than the Rose, and their cultivation is yearly extending, as it becomes more generally known that they are so easily grown, and that they can be procured at so trifling an expense. All that is necessary is to plant them in a bed of deep, fresh, loamy soil, well enriched with thoroughly rotted manure, and they are as certain to do well as a bed of Geraniums.

PREPARATION OF THE GROUND.—Roses will grow in any fertile ground, but are much improved in bloom, fragrance and beauty by rich soil, liberal manuring, and good cultivation. The ground should be subsoiled and well spaded to the depth of a foot or more, and enriched by digging in a good coat of cow manure or any fertilizing material that may be convenient. Renew old beds by decayed sods taken from old pasture land.

PLANTING.—When the ground is thoroughly prepared, fine and in nice condition, put in the plant slightly deeper than it was before, spread the roots out evenly in their natural position, and cover them with fine earth, taking care to draw it closely around the stem, and pack firmly down with the hand. It is very important that the earth be tightly firmed down on the roots. Budded Roses should be planted three inches below the bud. Always choose the most favorable time for planting in your own locality. Roses can be planted as soon as convenient after the frost is over. Always select an open, sunny place, exposed to full light and air. Roses appear to the best advantage when planted in beds or masses.

WATERING.—If the ground is dry when planted, water thoroughly after planting, so as to soak the earth down below the roots, and, if hot or windy, it may be well to shade for a few days.

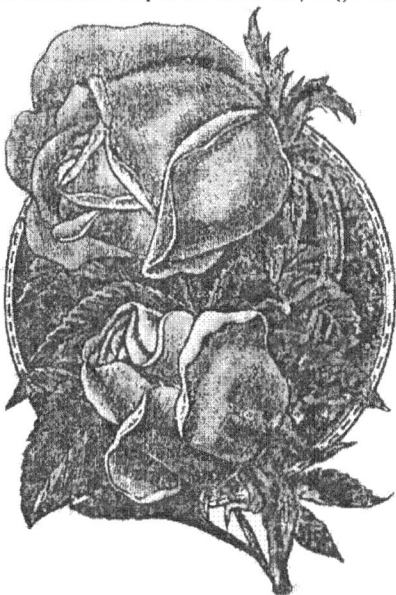

After this not much water is required unless the weather is unusually dry. Plants will not thrive if kept too wet and without drainage.

PRUNING.—In most seasons it is best to prune established plants of hardy kinds in February. Tender varieties, such as the Tea Roses and newly planted Roses, may be left till a month later. As a general rule close pruning produces quality, and long pruning quantity of bloom. Climbing, Weeping and Pillar Roses should not be cut back; but the tips of the shoots only should be taken off, and any weak or unripe shoots cut out altogether.

STANDARD LIST OF ROSES.

These Roses are all grown in two and one-half inch pots, and are from four to eight inches in height; they are vigorous and thrifty, grown especially for our mailing trade. We would like to have our list of Roses carefully examined, as it is without doubt the finest in the country. State what varieties you have, if selection is left to us, and we will not send them.

Price 10 Cents Each, $1.00 Per Dozen, Purchaser's Selection of Varieties, by Mail or Express. Our Selection, all Named from this List, SIXTEEN FOR ONE DOLLAR, by Mail or Express.

Aline Sisley. violet rose; a fruity, pleasant fragrance.

Arch Duke Charles. Brilliant crimson scarlet, shaded violet.

Antoine Verdier. Rich, dark, carmine pink, slightly shaded with white.

Adam. Bright flesh salmon rose, extra large size, double.

Adrienne Christopher. A lovely shade of apricot, citron and fawn.

Andre Schwartz. Beautiful crimson, free flowering variety.

Aurora. Creamy white, shaded dark rose and very double.

Arch Duchess Isabella. White, shaded with rosy carmine.

Agrippina. Rich velvety crimson. Few roses are so rich.

Apolline. A clear pink, dashed with rosy crimson.

Alba Rosea. Beautiful creamy white with rose-colored center.

Bella. Pure snow-white, splendid long, pointed buds. tea scent.

Bon Silene. Dark crimson rose, often changing to crimson.

Bougere. Bronzed pink, tinged with lilac. Large and full.

Belle Fleur de Anjou. Beautiful silver rose with pointed buds.

Beau Carmine. Fine carmine red, very rich, good size, double.

Baron Alexandre de Vrits. Delicate rose, highly perfumed.

Canary. Light canary yellow, beautiful buds and flowers.

Catherine Mermet. Its buds are inimitable, faultless in form, and charming in their every shade of color, from the purest silvery rose to the exquisite combining of yellow and rose, which illumes the base of the petals.

Cornelia Cook. The flowers are of the clearest, snowiest white, and are arranged in the most faultless and symmetrical manner.

Cels-Multiflora. Full and double, pale flesh, deepening to rose.

Charles Rovolli. A lovely shade of brilliant carmine.

Clement Nabonnand. Coppery rose, tinged purplish crimson.

Countess Riza du Parc. Coppery rose, tinged with soft violet.

Coquette de Lyon. A fine yellow rose, large, not at all formal.

Clara Sylvain. Creamy white, good, full form and fragrant.

Comtesse de Barbantine. Flowers large, beautifully cupped, full and very sweet.

Cloth of Gold, or Chromatella. A sulphur yellow of good substance and form; full and double; very sweet.

Crimson Bedder. Bright fiery red-velvety. Recommended.

Duchess de Brabant. A soft, light rose, with a heavy shading of amber and salmon.

Douglass. Dark cherry red, rich and velvety, large, full and double, fragrant.

Devoniensis. Magnolia Rose. Beautiful creamy white.

Duchess of Edinburgh. Buds of the most intense deep crimson.

Estella Pardell. Strong grower; fine buds of the purest white, with light yellow center; blooms in cluster.

Etoile de Lyon. Chrome-yellow, deepening to the center to pure golden-yellow, flowers very large and double.

Hermosa. Light pink; good bloomer.

Isabella Sprunt. This rose is sport from Safrano, which it resembles in all respects save in color, which is a bright canary yellow.

Jean Pernet. A beautiful pale yellow, suffused with salmon; of medium size; beautiful buds.

Jean Ducher. Yellow shaded salmon; a strong and vigorous grower; and a profuse bloomer.

La Nankin. Apricot yellow; fragrant; good form; very distinct.

La Sylphide. Blush, with fawn center; very large and double.

La Janquille. A saffron yellow; very distinct and always in bloom.

Lauretta. A blush white, with peach center, sometimes dotted with pink; very double and sweet.

La Princess Vera. A creamy white, bordered with coppery yellow; very full and sweet; a good new rose.

Lamarque. White, with yellow center; large, full flowered; very fragrant.

La Sylphide. Blush, with fawn center, very large and double.

La Tulip. Creamy white, tinted with carmine, full and fragrant.

Lady Warrender. Pure white, sometimes shaded with rose.

L'Elegante. Of vivid rose, center yellow, shaded with white.

Le Pactole. Elegant buds, color pale sulphur yellow.

Louis Phillipe. Rich dark velvety crimson, free and beautiful.

Lucullus. Beautiful dark crimson maroon. Full and fragrant.

Louis Richard. A coppery rose, beautifully tinted with lilac.

Louis de La Rive. A flesh-white, inclining to a rose center.

La Nuancee. Rose, tinged with fawn and coppery yellow.

La Chamoise. Nasturtium yellow. Very beautiful buds.

Mad. Berard. Apricot yellow; occasionally golden yellow; large and very double; of good substance and very sweet.

Mad. Celina Norey. A delicate shade of rose, the backs of petals purplish red; very large, full and of good habit.

Mad. La Countess de Casnerta. Coppery red flowers; large; petals of good substance, but not full; splendid buds for bouquets.

Mad. Louis Henry. Flowers medium to large silvery white; shaded yellow; fragrant and of good form.

Mad. Meline Vellermoz. Creamy white, thick petals, large and full, slightly fragrant; an excellent variety for planting out.

Mad. H. Jamin. White center, shaded yellow; large and full.

Marie Ducher. Vigorous and free grower; large, full flowers; color salmon with fawn center; a splendid variety.

Mareehal Niel. Bright golden yellow; very large, full and perfect form; of good substance. This is unquestionably the finest yellow rose grown.

Marshal Robert. White, center shaded with flesh; large, full and globular. 15 cents.

Molret. Pink shaded salmon; a very good rose.

Madamo Bravy. Creamy white, large, full and very symmetrical.

Madame Camille. Delicate rosy flesh, changing to salmon rose.

Madame Caroline Kuster. Bright lemon yellow and very large.

Madame Chedane Guinoiseau. A beautiful yellow rose with fine, long buds.

Madame Margettin. A beautiful citron yellow, coppery center.

Madame Maurice Kuppenhelm. Pale canary yellow, faintly tinged with pink.

Madame Pauline Labonte. Salmon rose, large and full.

Madame de Vatery. Red, shaded with salmon, of good form.

Marie Van Houtte. A lovely pale yellow color, with the oter petals most beautifully suffused with bright pink.

Madame Hippolite Jamain. White, yellow center, shaded pink.

Madame Jure. Lilac rose, good size and substance, fragrant.

Mademoiselle Raebel. A lovely Tea Rose, pure snow-white.

Marcelin Roda. Pale lemon yellow, lovely buds and flowers.

Mareehal Robert. Pure white, tinged and shaded rosy blush.

Maria Sisley. A pale yellow, margined with bright rose.

Madame Angele Jaequier. Light silvery rose, shaded yellow.

Madame Falcot. Deep apricot yellow, with fine orange buds.

Madame Dennis. Waxy white, center fawn and flesh, large.

Madame Dubroca. Delicate rose, shading to yellow.

Madame Lambard. Rosy bronze, changing to crimson.

Madame Welche. Pale yellow, sometimes cream, with short inner petals of glowing orange and copper.

Madame Brest. Rosy red, shaded to crimson, large flowers.

Marie Guillot. Holds first place among white Tea Roses, in purity of color, depth of petals, and queenliness of shape.

Madame Joseph Schwartz. White, beautifully flushed with pink, of good size; cupped, and borne in clusters.

Marie Duchere. Rich transparent salmon, with fawn center.

Madame Bosanquot. Flesh, shaded deep rose, large size, sweet.

Madame Damaizia. Salmon rose, changing to amaranth.

Monsieur Furtade. Yellow, well-formed, very full, fragrant.

Madame Joan Sisley. Pure white. An elegant rose.

Ma Capucine. Nasturtium yellow. Unique color.

Melville. Silvery pink. Bright and elegant.

THE BRIDE

Niphetos. A large and very double white rose of moderate growth; beautiful long pointed buds.

Perle des Jardins. Canary yellow; large, full, well formed; very fine. This undoubtedly is the best dwarf yellow rose in cultivation.

Perle de Lyon. Yellow, with salmon center; large, full, very fragrant.

Purple China. Rich, purplish crimson, velvety.

Pink Daily. Light pink flowers, produced in clusters.

Premium de Charrissions. Bright carmine rose, fawn center.

Queen's Scarlet. Dazzling crimson scarlet, has beautiful buds.

Queen of Bourbons. Clear carmine, changing to clear rose.

Robusta. Clear carnation red, veined rosy crimson.

Rol de Cramoisi. Bright purplish crimson, full and very double.

Regulus. Brilliant carmine, with purple and rose shading.

Rosa Nabonnand. Imbricated, delicate rose, vivid in center.

Rubens. A creamy white, with flesh center; very large and full; superb.

Reve d'Or. (Climbing Safrano.) Deep coppery yellow.

Solfatere. Sulphur yellow; large, double or full; fragrant; an excellent variety for the South.

Safrano. Bright apricot yellow, changing to orange and fawn.

Sombreuil. Beautiful white, tinged with delicate rose.

Souvenir de Madame Pernet. Beautiful, soft, silvery rose.

Sulphureaux. Sulphur yellow, fine in bud, fragrant.

Souvenir d'Elise Vardon. Creamy white, delicately shaded with pink, exceedingly fragrant.

Souvenir Isabelle Nabonnand. This is one of the most delicately colored roses; has large globular buds of a charming light fawn and silvery pink.

Souvenir de La Malmaison. A noble rose. The flower is extremely large, quartered and double to the center. Color, a flesh-white, clear and fresh. It has been considered the finest rose of its class for thirty years.

Sombreuil. This magnificent variety has immense finely formed flowers of beautiful white, tinged with delicate rose; buds large and full, blooming in clusters; a grand rose when in full bloom.

Souvenir d'un Amie. Rose, tinged with salmon; very large, full, highly perfumed; an old and reliable sort.

Souvenir du Mad. Pernet. A fine light rose color, shaded with yellow; a striking variety.

The Bride. The best pure ivory-white Tea Rose. The buds, which are of grand size, are carried high and erect on bright, smooth stems.

Triumph de Luxembourg. Rose carmine on a buff ground.

Ferle des Jardins.

Triumph de Luxemburg. A rosy carmine on a buff ground; an old rose and one of the best.

Vallee de Chamounix. The bask and back of the petals is a bright yellow, the center highly colored with glowing copper and rose every tint clear and bright.

White Bon Silene. This is a sprout from the old Bon Silene, possessing the same vigorous growth and free blooming qualities, differing only in color, being a pure pearly white.

White Daily. Pure white, beautiful long pointed buds.

Wm. Allen Richardson. Orange yellow, center a coppery yellow.

HYBRID TEAS AND HYBRID PERPETUALS.

All these Roses are grown in the open ground with us here, and are strong and vigorous. We could catalogue several hundred varieties of these Roses if we thought proper to do so, the list of them is so lengthy, but to save our customers confusion we catalogue only a limited number, all of which are good, and give the finest variety as to color, fragrance and form.

Price 25 Cents Each, $2.50 Per Dozen.

Abel Carrier. A very dark crimson, with violet shake; center bright red; large, full and double.

Alfred de Rougemont. Pure white; double and lasting.

Annie de Diesbach. Bright rose color; large and showy.

Beauty of Stapleford. A dark purplish crimson; flowers well formed and large; a very beautiful and distinct variety.

Caroline de Sansal. Pale flesh; large and full.

Coquette de Blanches. Pure white; large and full.

Duchess of Connaught. Most distinct in foliage and blooms; delicate silver rose with bright salmon center; large and highly scented.

Earl of Pembroke. Bright velvety crimson.

Empress of India. A dark violet crimson; double and fragrant; a splendid rose.

Francois Levot. Clear bright rose; fine grower.

Gen. Washington. Brilliant, rosy crimson; a good bloomer.

American Beauty.

Gen. Jacquminot. A velvety scarlet, changing to crimson; a free bloomer; good for winter forcing.

Hon. George Bancroft. Flowers large, full and regular; bright rosy crimson, shaded with purple; very beautiful.

John Hopper. Bright carmine; good.

Jules Margotton. Bright cherry red; large, well formed, fragrant flowers; double and free; splendid sort.

La Reine. Clear bright rose; of fine form.

Lord Bacon. Deep dark crimson, shaded with scarlet.

Mad. Alexandre Bernaise. Salmon rose, petals sometimes edged with blush; full and fragrant; a good variety.

Maria Bauman. Bright clear carmine; of perfect form; very fine.

La France. Peach shaded rose, that blooms through the winter season; double and fragrant. We consider this the finest rose known.

Nancy Lee. A satiny rose; a delicate and lovely shade; slender growth; flower medium or small; very fragrant.

Oxonian. A beautiful lilac rose, shaded crimson; very large, double and sweet.

Prince Camile de Rohn. Very deep velvety crimson; large and full; a good rose of splendid color.

Paul Neyron. Deep rose; very large and full; fragrant, free blooming; the largest variety known; very desirable.

Pride of Waltham. New; delicate flesh color, richly shaded with bright rose; very distinct; flowers large and full.

ROSES FROM FIVE INCH POTS.

We grow the following varieties in five inch pots. They are nice bushy plants, from twelve to eighteen inches high; were propagated last Spring and grown through the Summer and Fall in five inch pots.

Price 25 Cents Each; Our Selection, $2.50 Per Dozen.

Madame Ettenue.
Madame Schwaller.
Countess de Freigneuse
Chas. Rovolli.
Louis Richard.
Homer.
Mdll. Cecile Bruuner.
Adam.
Madame Dubrocea.
Madame Cusine.
Souv. de la Malmaison.
Ulrich Brunuer.
Mignonette.
Agrippina.
Marie Ducher.
Countess Laberth.

Andre Swartz.
La Pactole.
Marechal Neil.
La Janquille.
Paul Nabonnaud.
La Sylphide.
Perle des Jardins.
Mad Brest.
Aline Sisley.
Etoile de Lyon.
Bon Selene.
Hermosa.
Bougere.
Isabella Spruut.
Mad. Bravy.

Charles Rovolli.
Safrano.
Catherine Mermet.
Souvenir d'un Amie.
Croquette de Lyon.
Solfatere.
Mad. Joe Swartz.
Cornelia Cook.
La France.
Mad. Damazine.
La Princess Vern.
Mad. Lambard.
Marie Sisley.
Mad. Margotten.
Duchess of Edinburgh.

Louis de la Rive.
Queen's Scarlet.
Marie Guillott.
Sunset.
Pierre Guillott.
Mad. Cusin.
American Beauty.
Madame Camille.
Papa Gontier.
Marie Van Houtte.
Niphetos.
The Bride.
Mad. de Watteville.
Mad. Celine Berthod.
Bourbon Queen.

Large Size Roses.

NOISETTE AND TEA SCENTED.

For the past few seasons we have found an unusual demand for large Roses. Most people ordering want "plants that will bloom right away," and for the first time last season we offered this class of Roses with a great amount of satisfaction to each and every purchaser. This season we have an extra large stock and take pleasure in recommending them to all lovers of fine flowers. These Roses are grown in seven and eight inch pots, are very strong, and are cut back to two feet in height, of the following varieties.

Price 50 Cents Each, $5.00 Per Dozen.

Adam. Blush rose, salmon center.
..dele Jougeant. Clear yellow.
Adrienne Christophle. Yellow and white.
Aline Stanley. Purple rose to violet red.
Annie Oliver. Flesh colored rose.
Bele Lyonnaise. Yellow and salmon.
Bello Maconnaise. Light rose.
Bougere. Deep rosy bronze.
Bouquet d'Or. Deep yellow.
Bruct. Rosy purple.
Comte de Paris. Pale flesh.
Comte de Sembui. Salmon rose.
Comtesse La Barthe. Salmon pink.
Comtesse de Nadalliac. Bright rose.
Comtesse de Lyon. Cadury yellow.
Chromatella. Pale yellow.
Mons. Furtado. Sulphur yellow.
Montplaisir. Dark yellow, with salmon.
Narcisse. Pale yellow.

Niphet   Pure white.
Perfection de Montplaisir. Canary.
Perle de Lyon. Deep yellow.
Chromatella. Pale yellow.
Mons. Furtado. Sulphur yellow.
Montplaisir. Dark yellow, with salmon.
Narcisse. Pale yellow.
Niphetos. Pure white.
Perfection de Montplaisir. Canary.
Perle de Lyon. Deep yellow.
Porle des Jardins. Pale or canary yellow.
Reine Marie Henrietta. Reddish cerise.
Rove d'Or. Deep yellow or coppery.
Safrano. Apricot yellow to faint.
Devoniensis. Creamy white.
Duc de Magenta. Rosy salmon, with flesh.
Duchess des Cazes. Yellow.
Edouard Eduirer. Bluish cerise.
Enfant de Lyon. Pale yellow.

CLARKSVILLE, TENN. 15

Homer. White, with rose salmon center.
La Princess Vera. Copper, with yellow.
Mad. Berard. Fawn, with salmon,
Mad. Celine Noirey. Rose purple.
Mad. Denis. White, sulphur center.
Mad. Ducher. Clear yellow.
Mad. Falcot. Nankeen to yellow.
M'lle Mathilde Lenaerts. Rosy white.
Marechal Neil. Deep golden yellow.
Marie Ducher. Yellowish, with white rose.
Marie Guillot. White, with yellow.
Marie Van Houtte. Yellowish white.
Safrano a Fleur Rouge. Bluish cerise.
Shirley Hibb rd. Nankeen yellow.
Sombrieul. Pale lemon.

Solfaterre. Sulphur yellow.
Therese Loth. Bluish rose.
Triomphe de Rennes. Canary yellow.
Triomphe de Luxembourg. Buff rose.
Unique Jaune. Yellow, with vermillion.
William Allen Richardson. Yellow.
Zelia Pradel. White.
Malmaison. Fresh, shaded fawn; a beautiful rose.
Hon. Edith Gifford
Narcisse. Pale lemon yellow.
Niphetos. Pure white, pointed buds.
Jean Ducher. Bronzed rose.
Isabella Nabonnand
Mad. Eugene Verdier. Matted rose.

SIX SUPERB ROSES.

The following six Roses are unexcelled in the hardy Remontau class; each one is a beauty. They are not new, but we have yet to find their equal, not to say superior, among all the Roses of recent introduction. They are large, strong plants, that will flower beautifully this Summer. This set gives all the range of color to be found in this class of Roses, from the purest white through all the shades of pink to the richest velvety crimson.

Price 50 Cents Each, the Set of Six for $2.50.

Captain Christy. Flowers perfectly formed, of large size, and very double; of a delicate flesh color, slightly shaded salmon; constant bloomer; a gem.

La France. Peach shaded rose, that blooms through the whole season; double and fragrant. We consider this the finest rose grown.

Paul Neyron. Deep rose, very large and full, fragrant and free blooming. The largest variety known, and most desirable.

General Jacqueminot. This is the best known and most popular rose grown. It is perfectly hardy, free flowering, and very fragrant; color, dark brilliant crimson. This rose should be largely planted.

Baroness Rothschild. This might well be termed the "Queen of roses," as nothing can compare with the massive beauty of its flowers, which are five inches in diameter and an exquisite shade of satiny pink in color. The heavy foliage comes close up to the flowers, making a most effective background of green, thus giving the effect of a lovely bouquet rather than a single flower. It is perfectly hardy.

Mabel Morrison. A sport from Baroness Rothschild. Flesh, changing to pure white; in the autumn tinged with rose; double, cup shaped flowers freely produced. It is the most beautiful white hybrid perpetual raised.

SIX OLD STAND-BYS.

To the exclusion of many of the novelties now catalogued in glowing colors, we here offer our "six old stand-by" Roses, nothing new by any means, but good old Roses of the Tea and ever-blooming persuasion, with good clear records for growing vigorously, flowering abundantly, and pleasing everybody with their beautiful blossoms. We recommend these especially to anybody who has not already got them, or to parties not familiar with Roses and want a good reliable selection to start with. They are large, strong plants, that will come into bloom soon after planting.

Price 50 Cents Each, the Set of Six $2.50.

Marie Van Houtte. Yellowish white, outer petals pink.
Sombreuil. Pale lemon.
Safrano. Apricot yellow.

Triomph of Luxemburg. Buff rose.
Devoniensis. Cream white.
Malmaison. Flesh, changing to pink; a gem.

Two Fine Roses for the South.

Last Spring we sold more Wm. Allen Richardson Roses than any other one variety we catalogued, except Marechal Niel. It is a beautiful Rose, and growing in favor more each day as it becomes known. It is a beautiful shade of yellow, of a deep bronze tint, a running Rose, and fine for porches or arbors. Belle Lyonaise is another fine companion Rose, a climber also, very vigorous, a pale yellow, fine strong wood, and handsome foliage. These two would make a handsome pair for a porch or door yard, or for greenhouse and pit culture. Very strong. Price 50 cents each.

LARGE GRAFTED ROSES.

For some years past we have had a continual demand for large grafted plants of Marechal Niel, Glorie de Dijon, Lamarque, etc., for planting in conservatories, pits and greenhouses, or out-door planting in the Southern States, and we are glad to be able to offer some excellent ones. They are grafted on stout, well grown stocks, and about five feet high. We can highly recommend them. We have the following varieties, which we offer at $1.50 each:

Marechal Neil.	Mad. Elsie Rochford.	Cloth of Gold.	Mad. Mathilda Lan-
Glorie de 'Dijon.	Ketten Freres.	Lamarque.	erts.
Wm. Allen Richardson	Homer	Celine Forester.	Archduchess Marta Im-
Belle Lyonaise.	Unique Jaune.	Triomph de Rennes.	maculata.
Reine M. Henrietta.			

MARECHAL NIEL ROSES.

We have undoubtedly the finest stock of this popular Rose in the country, ranging in price from 10 cents to $1.50 each, according to size, both grafted and on their own roots. Our 50 cent plants are fine; have them with buds on, and also in dormant condition; are from two and one-half to three and four feet high, and we highly recommend them and guarantee satisfaction. Price, according to size, 10, 25 and 50 cents, and $1.50.

New and Scarce Roses.

We offer the following new and scarce Roses. We have tried them and consider them an acquisition to existing varieties.

Nice Young Plants. 50 Cents Each.

Dr. Grill. Medium size, vivid yellow, center light orange, shaded pink; exquisite fragrance.

Luciole. Very bright carmine rose, tinted and shaded saffron; base coppery; buck of petals bronze; large and full; finely scented; good shape; long buds.

M'me Scipion Cochet. In bud yellowish pink, banded flesh rose, center yellowish; very free bloomer.

Meteor. Hybrid Tea, of strong bushy growth; producing qualities of finely formed deep crimson; scarlet flowers; very free and productive.

Mad. de Watteville. This grand rose is one of the most beautiful varieties lately introduced. The color is a remarkable shade of creamy yellow, richly tinged with carmine, while the large shell like petals each have a wide border of bright crimson. The flowers are finely rayed, large; very full and highly perfumed.

Papa Gontier. Extra large, finely formed buds and flowers; full and fragrant and very beautiful; color a brilliant carmine, changing to pale rose; reverse of petals fine purplish red.

M'me Francisca Kreuger. Extra fine, orange yellow, tinted rose.

Madame Etienne. Called in France the Dwarf Mermet. It is a rose of great promise. Very free producing its buds on short, stout stems.

M'me. Hon. Defresno. Beautiful dark citron yellow, with coppery reflex; charming as as bud as well as open flower; strong grower; free bloomer.

Chateau des Bergories. A large canary yellow bud, nearly equal to Perle in size; recommended by its raisers as a winter forcing variety.

Duchess do Bragrance. Light canary yellow. After the style of Coquette de Lyons, but stronger, and of better construction.

Sou. de Wooton. An American variety of great promise for forcing purposes and it is being largely planted by cut flower men. Color rosy crimson, or crimson red.

The Queen. A most charming white sport from Sou. d' un Ami, will be useful for white flowers. We esteem this highly.

Mme. Schwaller. This rose has the strong, firm growth of the H. P's, the same form and finish of flower, being especially beautiful when full grown. The color is a bright rosy flesh, paler at the base of the petals.

Princess Beatrice. A most beautiful rose, and will be of value to all florists for summer buds. Splendid for pots; fine for bedding.

Four Excellent Roses.

AMERICAN BEAUTY.

CATHERINE MERMET.

THE BRIDE.

PERLE DES JARDINS.

In our estimation these four Roses have no superiors as everbloomers. Perle des Jardins is the best yellow; Bride, the best white; Beauty, the best red, and Catherine Mermet, the best pink. Thus you have four distinct Roses, the best in their respective colors, that we can well recommend. Price for the four, one strong plant of each, $1.00.

CHRYSANTHEMUMS.

Lilian B. Bird.

There is no more popular flower at the present day than the Chrysanthemum. There is more interest manifested in its culture than any other flower we cultivate; even the Rose, the all acknowledged "Queen of Flowers," has to take a second place during the season the Chrysanthemums are in bloom. Through the month of November, go where you will, you will find in almost any city or town that has any pretentions to culture and refinement, a Chrysanthemum show. It is not more than eight years ago since the first display of this kind was held in New York, and now they are widespread over the land. These shows do much to advance the interest in this class of plants, and if the interest continues to increase within the next few years as it has done for some years past, it is difficult to say what may be obtained, as each season sees some improvement over the past in some of the new varieties that are continually coming forth, and the old ones known to our grandmothers have well nigh vanished from the scene.

OUR CHRYSANTHEMUM SHOW.

A number of ladies of this city have formed themselves into an organization known as "The Ladies' Confederate Monumental Association," their worthy object being to raise sufficient funds to erect a monument in our city in memory of the Confederate soldiers killed in the late war, many of whom lie buried in this vicinity. To assist in this laudable work, as soon as our Chrysanthemums were in bloom we turned our entire place over to the ladies interested for a period of two weeks. They had full charge of the entire place, and charged an

admission fee for enter-
ing the large conserva-
tory where the display
of Chrysanthemums was
held, and were allowed
also a commission on all
the sales of plants, bulbs
and flowers they were in-
strumental in making.
The result was that for
two weeks our gardens
were in gala attire, and
visited daily by hundreds
of people, many of whom
came long distances to
see them, and all went
away surprised and de-
lighted at the beauty of
the display, having little
idea before coming that
the Chrysanthemum con-
tained such a vast array
of color and wonderful
diversity of formation.
The entire vocabulary of
adjectives would be ex-
hausted before they got
one-fourth the way through the house. We are confident no exhibition of this
kind in the country attracted such widespread interest as ours, and nowhere
could a finer assortment be found. We only wished that all our customers had
an opportunity to see them, as a scene of this kind cannot be properly described, but must be seen to be believed. The press of the country around us
was full of it, and we append but a few of the notices:

Courier-Journal, Louisville, Ky.

A chrysanthemum show is being held in
Clarksville under the auspices of the Ladies
Confederate Monumental Association. The
display of flowers is the finest in the country,
and is visited by hundreds daily.

Farmers Home Journal, Louisville, Ky.

Judging from the fact that excursion trains
are being run to Clarksville to convey large
crowds to the chrysanthemum show, now being held there, and such a great amount of
interest manifested in the culture of this particular plant that we think it ought to be
adopted as our national flower.

Bowling Green, Ky. Democrat.

Mr. W. C. Alexander visited the chrysanthemum show at Clarksville yesterday, and was
charmed with the endless variety and exquisite beauty of the display. He advises all
his friends to go and see, they will never regret it.

A young lady writing to the Princeton, Ky.
Banner, says: "I have never seen any chrysanthemums except the common ones that
every one has, so I could hardly believe my
eyes when I entered the room devoted to
them and saw the superb mass of colors. Mr.
Morton, the head gardener, told me they have
three hundred varieties. They are of every
color, size and shape, and I wish I could give
you even a faint idea of their beauty. There
are pure white and deep cream, pale lemon
and deep yellow, pink, magenta, garnet and
purple. There were some so curly that they
looked like they were made of crimpled paper
and others with sharp pointed petals like
porcupine quills. Some I noticed had long
outside leaves and the centers were filled with

what looked like hundreds of the tiniest
blossoms, each one perfect in itself. The most
beautiful ones of all were a white one with
leaves at least three inches long, having
irregular stripes of lavender, and another
equally as large, having the upper sides of its
leaves bright yellow and the under sides dark
red."
"I heard a gentleman say yesterday: 'Oh,
chrysanthemums don't amount to anything;
my mother has a dozen varieties in her yard.'
If he could once see these he would change
his mind."

Daily Tribune, Rome, Ga.

Yesterday afternoon Mr. O. H. McWilliams
brought to The Tribune office a large basket
containing 26 chrysanthemum blossoms, displayed a glorious perfection. They were
especially noted for their size, as they were
the largest ever seen in Rome. Among them
were rich cream, velvet red, golden brown,
white lilacs, and other brilliant blossoms
making a delicious harmony in color. This
elegant collection was sent to Mr. McWilliams by J. J. Crusman, of Clarksville, Tenn.
The basket of blossoms will be on exhibition
at Brazer & Tanner's book store to-day until
noon. They are well worth a visit to see.

Owensboro, Ky. Messenger.

Last summer some of the ladies of Clarksville, Tenn., with Mrs. Clark at their head,
organized an association for the purpose of
making money to erect a monument in hon-
or of the Confederate soldiers who are buried
there. Capt. J. J. Crusman, owner of Evergreen Lodge, a greenhouse, offered the ladies
the use of his greenhouse for a chrysanthemum fair, as during November his chrysanthemums are at their best. During the past
week different railroads gave reduced rates.

Tuesday there was an excursion from Nashville, Wednesday there were parties from Elkton, Bowling Green and Russellville, and Thursday from Princeton and Hopkinsville. Each day the ladies of the association met the guests with carriages and took them to the greenhouse.

Clarksville Daily Progress.

Yesterday the great chrysanthemum show, of which so much has been said and written in the last month, was opened with all the eclat that so important an occasion demanded. The weather was perfect, as if nature itself smiled on the noble object of the Ladies' Monumental Association, and lavished on their fete all her riches of blue and gold autumnal days.

Up at Evergreen Lodge, where the flower show is to be held, everything was in gala attire. The air was heavy with the spicy sweetness of chrysanthemums, with here and there a breath of belated roses, the crisp wind flaunted the stars and stripes in the breeze from a dozen flagstaffs, a pretty little platform for the orator had been erected fronting a gentle declivity and tastefully decorated with masses of potted plants, there were animated groups of pretty women strolling about the lovely grounds, and altogether it looked more like a big garden party than anything else.

But the chrysanthemums themselves were naturally the first object of interest, for it is a well-known fact that Capt. Crusman's collection is the finest in the South, if not indeed this side of New York. One whole greenhouse has been set apart and no money or pains is spared to get and propagate the finest specimens of this royal flower of Japan. In front of this long conservatory, just by the door through which one catches tantalizing glimpses of billowy masses of bloom, is the headquarters of the Ladies' Monumental Association, and where they have encamped under a banner bearing the significent legend: "There are no tears more holy than those shed by weeping beauty at the grave of vanquished valor." Within among the flowers is a green bank of encti on which is picked out in purple immortelles the sentence that strikes the key note of all the association has done and hopes to do: "In memory of C. S. A., they bravely fought and bravely fell."

It is like a minor chord, that phrase in all this brightness and gladness, for the air is full of gay laughter, there are hundreds of flags above one's head, the star and crescent of the Orient, sacred dragons, and the ensigns of far Japan, and about all the delicious, penetrating odor of the flower whose feast of beauty is being celebrated.

One who remembers the little bunch of chrysanthemums in some quiet country garden is a little bewildered by all this prodigality of bloom and beauty. There they are in rank and file of loveliness, white, red, yellow, pink, mauve, they run the whole gamut of color. Here is one like a snow-drift out of time—eight inches it measures across its deep fringed fronds, here is another red as if dipped in blood, here another you could swear is a wild aster from a Northern brook, and here is still another that with its deep, mysterious blending of a hundred colors looks as some priceless orchid might in its far off tropical home.

You might spend a day among them, still unsatisfied, until you forget this is not Tokio and the fair maid who is your patient guide not some Yum-Yum standing at home among her own flowers in Japan.

But already the band was beginning to play on the lawn and coming up in a column that was rather more ragged than it used to be when it faced the enemy's smoking batteries was Forbes Bivouac. There was a cheer for the veterans and then Capt. Crusman, acting

as master of ceremonies, introduced Rev. Dr. A. D. Sears, the chaplain of Forbes Bivouac, who delivered a short prayer, invoking divine guidance and assistance in the matter about to be inaugurated. At the close of the prayer Capt. Crusman introduced the handsome and eloquent orator of the day, Hon. Joe Washington, member of congress from this district, who spoke with a directness and earnest eloquence that charmed his audience.

Clarksville Daily Chronicle.

The opening exercises of the chrysanthemum show were highly interesting and were largely attended. The crowd was variously estimated at 200 to 500 people.

The grounds were decorated with rare flowers and with United States flags. A banner at the entrance to the hot-house containing the chrysanthemums, bears the following inscription: "There are no tears more holy than those of weeping beauty at the grave of vanquished valor."

The Hon. Jas. A. McKenzie was asked for a suitable inscription for the banner, and the above beautiful and touching one was suggested by him.

A stage was erected on the lawn in the inclosure and was beautifully trimmed off with flowers and tropical plants.

Forbes Bivouac formed a line of march at the court-house about 2 o'clock, headed by the C. C. G. drum corps and Hayden's brass band marched out to the Lodge, where the crowd was addressed by the Hon. Jos. E. Washington. The gentleman spoke briefly but eloquently. He paid the members of Forbes Bivouac a tribute in his flowery style, and turning to the ladies he poured out a stream of eloquent praise that thrilled every bosom with rapture, and every heart with patriotism.

After the speaking the crowd was invited to visit the display of beauty characteristic of Evergreen Lodge—the chrysanthemums. Several hundred people marched up and deposited their dimes and took a look at the flowers. The general verdict was that it was the finest display ever seen in the South.

Clarksville Democrat.

There is not we presume, in the entire country, any city that is more interested in chrysanthemums than Clarksville is to day. Special trains and a large concourse of people is the order of the day. Soldiers in uniform, a brass band, drum corps, and about 250 of Tennessee and Kentuck's fairest daughters from the Clarksville Female Academy, helped to make things gay out there yesterday. Superintendent Morton says, pretty girls, pretty flowers and sweet music, is all on earth that's worth living for—these blessings he now enjoys to his heart's content.

Nashville Daily American.

A party of ladies and their friends left Nashville yesterday by special train to visit the chrysanthemum exhibition at Clarksville. This display is the finest in the country, the entire place being one vast bed of flowers and the largest floral gardens anywhere in the South. The ladies were charmed with all they saw—of the beauty of the chrysanthemums, they say the half can never be told. Capt. Crusman not only threw his charming residence open to them, but tore the latch strings completely away. A sumptuous dinner was served, and the remainder of the evening was spent strolling through the lawns and green-houses—it was a most enjoyable ocassion, that all those who were fortunate enough to be present will never forget. Another excursion is fixed for Friday.

Cullingfordii.

OUR LIST OF VARIETIES.

We publish this season four separate lists of varieties. The first list contains all the newest and finest to date, selected with the greatest care. There is a couple of dozen other new varieties upon the market this season, which we do not offer, believing they have not been sufficiently tested. The set of six new ones we offer we know to be good, and offer them only on that account. These have been selected when in bloom from among the other new varieties we do not offer. The varieties in the twenty-five cent list needs no commendation from all who saw them in bloom last Fall; every one is a beauty and cheap at the price named. The ones in the fifteen cent list are as yet all scarce varieties, but every one of them is fine. The general list needs no words of praise to all familiar with good Chrysanthemums.

Newest and Finest Chrysanthemums to Date.

This is the best set of strictly American seedlings ever sent out by any one. Single plants $1.00 each, the collection of six varieties for $5.00. Ready for distribution March 1st:

Ada Spaulding. A striking novelty; without question the finest introduction of the year; neither Japanese nor Chinese form, but globe shaped; a new type; has been exhibited 7½ inches in depth by 6¼ in diameter; habit most sturdy and robust; color novel and distinct, the lower half of the flower being a rich deep pink, shading in upper portion to the purest pearl white; petals very large, broad and solid; awarded at Indianapolis the National prize for best seedling, a silver cup presented by Mrs. President Harrison, also certificate of merit and silver medal by Pennsylvania Horticultural Society, first premium from the New Jersey Floriculture Society, and medal of excellence by American Institute, New York.

E. G. Hill. Immense bloom of brightest golden yellow; full and very double; lower petals sometimes deeply shaded bright carmine; an elegant variety of strong habit; awarded certificate of merit at Indianapolis and medal by the Pennsylvania Horticultural Society.

Garnet. A showy Japanese variety; inner side of petals a rich wine red, reverse silvery pink; on first opening petals have a peculiar manner of twisting or curling, showing the reverse color, when fully expanded they display the red shade.

Mrs. Thos. A. Edison. A large incurved flower with compact center; one mass of long petals of the most delicate rose pink; very free, large, and so closely incurved as to resemble a solid ball; certificate of merit awarded by the New Jersey Floricultural Society.

G. P. Rawson. A superb double variety; very large; of an entirely new shade of rich buff with center petals of bright nankeen and apricot yellow; broad, nearly erect, and slightly whorling; a magnificent variety.

Marie Ward. A grand and beautiful cup shaped variety, very double, and of large size; color purest snow white; petals very long and somewhat narrow; a sport from Mrs. J. N. Gerard, with which it is identical, except in color; a fine exhibition variety.

New English Chrysanthemum, "Mrs. S. Coleman."

This is an English importation controlled by parties here, and said to be the finest of all Chinese varieties yet introduced. Color clear canary yellow, reverse of petals uniformly striped with rose and apricot shades. Flowers large and deep, one of the grandest novelties of the strictly incurved type. No exhibition collection complete without it. National Societies first-class certificate at London, also first-class certificates at Birmingham, Liverpool, Hull, Manchester, York, Sheffield and Bristol, England. Price $1.50 each. Ready March 1st.

New Set of American Raised Varieties for 1890.

All prize winners. Price $1.00 each, the set of twelve for $10.00. Ready March 1st:

Harry E. Widener. Winner of the Blanc prize at the Philadelphia show, November last, "for the best seedling plant." This is unquestionably the variety of the year, and unequaled in its color by any. Bright lemon yellow in color, without shadings. Flower large, on stiff, stout stems that hold the flowers erect, without support; incurving, forming a large rounded surface; petals crisp and stiff, very free in growth, but not coarse. This is the cut flower variety, and all that could be desired in the way of good color, fine form, and lasting qualities.

Mrs. J. T. Emlen. Deep blood red on upper surface of the petals, under side old gold. A very large incurved flower of most splendid shape. Considered a great improvement over Mrs. A. Carnagle, both in size, color and form.

Molly Bawn. Those acquainted with Syringa will need no word of praise for its sport, Mollie Bawn. It is pure white, having been grown two years, which shows its color to be fixed. A most valuable variety, for its size, shape and purity.

Robert S. Brown. A magnificent dark crimson like Hon. John Welsh in color, but four times as large. Will make a magnificent exhibition variety, either as a cut flower or grown in pots. Fine grower and very free bloomer. Color richest crimson, very bright and attractive.

Mrs. Mary Weightman. A magnificent and very distinct chrome yellow, in form loose and feathery, but very large and full. The flowers are ten inches across, early. One of the best commercial and exhibition sorts.

Crown Prince. Another of Mr. Monahan's productions. A splendid improvement on Mrs. C. H. Wheeler, with broader petals, and of a deeper hue of color. One-third larger than any in its class. Color ox-blood red on upper surface; old gold beneath.

Clara Riemen. Certificate of merit by the National Chrysanthemum Committee at the Indianapolis show. A rich lavender rose in color, shading to silvery rose, with white centre. A very large open surfaced flower of fine texture.

John Lane. Raised by William K. Harris, and purchased by us. A magnificent pink ball in appearance; fine for pots, splendid for cutting. Color, a rose pink, with peach or light shadings on under side of petals, ends of centre petals tipped with gold. Flowers borne on long, stiff, stout stems. An ideal cut flower variety in every respect, but equally as good for exhibition purposes. Considered a grand novelty.

Charles A. Reeser. A novel and peculiar shade of color, quite distinct; a violet pink, without shadings. A fine recurved variety of good habit. Splendid for pots, making a fine exhibition plant.

Mrs. Winthrop Sargeant. Brilliant straw color, incurved, carrying its flowers on long, stiff stems. Very large, if not the largest in this line of color.

Carrie Denny. Clear amber, entirely distinct from anything in cultivation. A most novel and striking color. Comes in large spherical balls, incurving and slightly whorled. This beautiful variety is named for the wife of ex-Mayor Denny, of Indianapolis, who so graciously opened the Chrysanthemum show at that city.

Mrs. Edmund Smith. A beautiful pure white, of an entirely new type of flower. Pure white, long narrow petals, of great substance and lasting quality; petals beautifully interlaced; entirely new type; an exquisite thing.

New Chrysanthemums of Last Season.

We have grown the following last season, and can highly recommend them. Every one is a beauty. Price, the set of twelve varieties for $3.00, by mail or express:

Mrs. Andrew Carnegie. The best seedling Chrysanthemum ever offered in America or Europe; bright deep crimson, reverse of petals a shade lighter; broad, long and flat; of leathery texture, incurving on first opening, afterwards assuming the form of a large peony; strong, erect, heavy foot stalks; of robust habit, and a prize winner wherever exhibited. 25 cts.

Mrs. W. K. Harris. Deepest rich golden yellow, thoroughly incurved, probably the best yellow Chrysanthemum ever raised; in the way of Grandiflorum, but far larger and better than that variety. It is certainly the finest yellow variety in cultivation for cut flowers or exhibition. 50 cts.

Mrs. Alpheus Hardy. The most sensational novelty was the beautiful Mrs. Alpheus Hardy. Words are inadequate to convey an idea of its beauty. The flowers are pure white, medium size, incurved Japanese, the centre slightly indented, the disc entirely hidden; on the upper surface of the floret petals is what at first sight appears hoar frost or snow, which gives it a chaste, delicate and fluffy appearance. A silver medal was awarded to the introducers of this grand Chrysanthemum at the Philadelphia show in November. There has been more written about this variety than any yet introduced. 25 cts.

Lilian B. Bird. Came in the same set with Mrs. Hardy. Of the very largest size, with full, high center; petals tubular, and of varying lengths; the flower when fully open being an immense half globe; the color is an exquisite shade of "shrimp pink." 35 cts.

Wm. H. Lincoln. A magnificent golden yellow variety, with straight, flat, spreading petals. An extra large flower, completely double, and of great substance. 25 cts.

Luecroe. Pure white, resembling Christmas Eve, but surpassing that in size, form and lateness; largely used for cutting and late decorations. 15 cts.

Miss Esmeralda. Incurved, deep crimson; double flowers; well built; tips of petals have a decided silvery tinge; lower row of petals flat red coppery bronze. This is a grand and strong variety for decoration or exhibition. 20 cts.

Alice Bird. A large, compact and well formed flower of intensely bright buttercup yellow, somewhat deeper in centre; one of the finest yellow varieties yet raised. Two first-class certificates. 25 cts.

The Bride. This was disseminated last year without its intrinsic worth being known; a season's trial has demonstrated its value, and it has been placed at the head of all white varieties. Those who want the finest white Chrysanthemum in cultivation must invest in The Bride. 25 cts.

Kioto. A beautiful incurved yellow of fine form and habit; no collection complete without it. 25 cts.

Nymphcea. A new sweet scented variety, the flowers resembling a water lily, hence its name; has a most pleasing fragrance; a vigorous grower and a fine acquisition to any collection. 25 cts.

Lady Trevor Lawrence. An exquisite white, with broad incurved petals, a large flower and compact grower. 25 cts.

New and Scarce Chrysanthemums.

The following list contains the best of all the French and English importations of the past two years. Also the cream of American seedlings, all of which are yet scarce. Price 15 cents each, $1.50 per dozen, by mail or express. The forty-two varieties for $4.00:

Alaska. A beautiful snow white.

Adriondac. Round, full petalled; white.

Alcyon. Deep rose, shaded lilac, outer petals reflexed, centre incurved, silvery white; fine flower of good habit.

Aspasia. A large symmetrical flower with broad petals; outer florets soft pale satiny rose, centre purplish rose.

Baronald. A variety vieing with G. F. Moseman in beauty and size; flowers large, deep red and bronze.

Bettina. Beautiful clear bronze, incurved, large flowers and long petals.

Belle Poitevine. Large spherical snow white, the most regular and perfect incurved.

O. Wagstaff. Pure white; the best of Japanese type.

Capancine. Center brownish yellow, incurved, a very large half globe.

Cythere. Bright rosy violet, immense flower in ball shape, and of even coloring.

Excellent. Soft pink, resembling the color of a Mermet Rose; very double.

Elkshorn. An extra large incurved flower of soft pearl color; after incurving towards the centre, the petals, which are nearly tubular, rise, and from the tips three gracefully farmed branches arch upward; an exquisite variety in both color and form.

Herman Payne.

Leopard. The only spotted variety extant.

L. Canning. A most exquisite white, absolutely pure; the flower is quite regular in form, very large and flat, the length of petals graduating to the centre; a little later than Puritan, to which it is a grand successor; reminds one of a large satin rosette.

Lambeth. Early, dwarf, and of strong habit; purest white, and one of the largest early double varieties; flowers five to six inches across, borne in clusters.

Little Tycoon. Very large flowers; marbled with rose; petals broad and irregular in form, the centre ones incurving; fine.

Louis Wellie. Large flowers; violet mauve, lighter centre.

Ada Spaulding.

La Dauphinois. Enormous flower, very double; yellow ochre, brightening as the flower opens; a very choice variety of good habit; first-class certificate.

Montplaisant. Petals incurved; crimson red at base, golden yellow at extremity; fine for bush plants.

Mrs. Anthony Wiegand. Beautiful rich pink; a decided improvement in this line of color; form excellent; producing flowers in great abundance.

Mrs. Richard Elliott. Another grand yellow, in every way distinct from Mrs. Price and Mrs. May; the form is regular, very double, showing no centre, very large, and slightly recurved; petals long, and of medium width; a grand exhibition variety.

Mrs. Howells. A very fine red and gold variety; outer petals broad and velvety and reflexed; inner petals incurved, forming a round golden ball; very brilliant; a fine show variety.

Mrs. DeWitt Smith. Beautiful soft rose, changing to white at the centre.

Mrs. M. J. Thomas. Of the purest white, without shade or stain; incurved so that no centre shows; the petals are very broad, of the heaviest texture, and tightly incurved; a massive flower of great size and substance.

Magnet. An immense drooping flower of reddish Heliotrope color; most generally admired.

Monadnoc. Tubular petalled yellow; of fine form.

Mrs. J. C. Price. An improved form of Golden Dragon; very handsome.

Mr. H. Connoll. Style of Grandiflora, but far richer and broader; petals incurved of the most lovely shape; color richest possible yellow.

Mrs. Anthony Waterer. An immense spreading flower which has been produced eleven inches across, the individual petals being one and a quarter inches; at first very pale blush on outside, which that it loses as it matures; when fully expanded, has the appearance of a bunch of white ribbon.

Mme. Drexel. A large Japanese variety in the general style of Mrs. Frank Thompson; the flower is more incurved and the habit more compact; of vigorous growth, and a very free bloomer; outside of petal silvery white, inside bright pink at the tips, shading to white at the centre; holds finely in bloom, and lasts well when cut.

Mrs. J. N. May. Exactly like Mrs. Thomas, except in color, which is a soft clear yellow; these two are fine companion pieces, flowering at the same time.

Mrs. E. W. Clark. Splendid, good size, of extra fine form ; deep amaranth purple, reflex silvery rose; one of the finest varieties extant; special premium at Indianapolis and special prize at Philadelphia.

Mrs. A. Blanc. Centre of floret erect; outer petals horizontal or drooping, of rosy lavender, center soft clear rose, with a touch of gold in centre; an exquisite rosy flower and good grower.

Naragansett. Reflexed clear white flower with white centre.

Ramona. Bright amber color.

Phidias. Blush pink and silvery white; incurved.

Ralph Broklebank. A sport from Meg Merriluse ; yellow, flat petals of irregular form.

Seuzon. Clear yellow, very brilliant.

Sabine. Soft canary yellow, of exactly the form of Timbale de Argent, that is a medium sized Anemone.

Veil d'Or. Beautiful Japanese, yellow, broad petals; incurved and distinct.

Walter W. Coles. Very bright reddish terra cotta, reverse pale yellow ; outer petals long, broad, pointed and horizontal; centre short petals, bright gold folded into pointed threads, and whorled ; a very large flower, and exquisitely beautiful.

Christmas Eve.

WHEN TO BUY CHRYSANTHEMUMS.

We are often asked, "what is the best time to buy Chrysanthemums," and to all such we say right now is the best, as a plant that you can purchase now for ten cents by Fall will be worth fifty cents or more ; also at this season the plants are small, and a dozen can be sent now for less than one plant could be transported in the Fall. As they are vigorous growers they may be set out at once and will grow into large plants before Fall.

General Collection of Chrysanthemums.

The varieties enumerated in this list are all good. Among them will be found most of the novelties that were prize winners at the various shows last Fall. Price from this list 10 cents each, purchaser's selection ; fifteen for $1.00 ; our selection, twenty for $1.00 :

Albert Delaux. Very large fine flowers; petals large, incurved, silvery white ; reverse tender rose.

Areguine. Good old bronze variety of great merit.

Alba Plena. Compact double white ; early and good.

Alleghana. Fine white large petals resembling Carnation.

Agnes Hamilton. Beautiful rose and pink.

Bessie Fitcher. Deep rose pink with lighter centre ; a grand flower.

Ben d'Or. Handsome twisted yellow.

Bruce Findlay. Rich lemon yellow; a sport from Emily Dale.

Bould de Neigh. Fine white compact flowers; a very free bloomer.

Bicolor. Large flat flowers, red, striped orange, late.

Baron de Prally. Extra large flower; white, striped with lilac.

Bronze Jardin des Plantes. Bronze sport from Jardin des Plantes ; fine show flower.

Bronze Queen of England. A bronze sport from Queen of England ; extra fine.

Boule Canaise. Dwarf ; bright yellow.

Citron. Yellow, free and late.

Christmas Eve. Magnificent white of greatest beauty.

Christine. Peach, fine and distinct.

Comte de Germiny. Bright yellow, broad petals, shaded bronze.

Charlotte de Montcabrier. Silvery white, with silvery rose centre; long petals, tufted.

Cullingfordii. Rich crimson, shaded scarlet ; very large reflexed flowers, beautiful and distinct ; this is the finest scarlet variety in existence.

Coquette. Petals twisted, gilded mahogany ; yellow.

Duck of Teck. Rosy mauve, suffused white ; distinct.

Diana. One of the best whites.

Duke of Berwick. Petals twisted, milky white, veined.

Duchess of Manchester. The best white Chinese variety in cultivation.

Diana. Small white ; free and good.

Domination. A grand variety ; flowers creamy white, large and fine ; early and very handsome.

Etincelle. Red, shaded maroon, and pointed golden yellow ; flowers very large ; a beautiful variety, much esteemed.

Edouard Andigier. One of the finest of recent introduction ; of enormous size ; in color a rich velvety purple violet, with a silvery reverse ; a shade scarcely to be found in this family.

Eugene Mezard. Amaranth ; reverse of petals violet white, forming a ball at the centre; very fine.

E. S. Renwick. Silvery blush, reflexed ; large size and fine.

Elaine. Pure white, broad petals, very fine.

Eva. Salmon, white and pink; flowers quite large ; an acquisition.

Empress of India. Pure white sport from Queen of England ; of same character.

Emily Dale. Rich primrose; flowers of large size and fine form; one of the best, incurved.

Frank Wilcox. Flower with very erect petals, slightly toothed, above medium size ; rich golden amber, slightly shaded deep bronze; one of the best to last.

Fantasia. Cream white, pure and distinct.

Fair Maid of Guernsey. Flowers very large, of the snowiest white, in clusters; one of the best.

Fabias de Medina. Anemonic flowered ; high centre.

F. L. Harris. Bright crimson red, a new and fine color; distinct and good.

F. T. McFadden. A reflexed Japanese with immense flowers, having broad, flat petals ; the color is a rich mauve purple, an entirely new shade, and most desirable ; will be a fine variety for specimens.

Fleur Parfaite. Rose tinted lilac ; flowers large and early.

Frizou. Pure golden yellow ; large flowers, with centre petals whorled.

Gloriosum. Very light lemon, with immense flowers, having narrow petals most gracefully curved and twisted ; well merits its name, and is one of the most attractive varieties we have ever grown.

Golden Rayonnante. A charming yellow variety of most beautiful color; flowers large, and borne in immense clusters; early.

Golden Queen. Fine deep yellow, large and late; a great bloomer.

Golden Dragon. Yellow, with long twisted petals ; one of the richest and handsomest colors.

Gorgeous. Golden yellow ; a magnificent variety, early and distinct.

Grandiflorum. A magnificent variety ; flowers of immense size, often six inches in diameter; petals very broad, incurving, so as to form a solid ball of the purest golden yellow ; one of the very finest, no collection complete without it.

George A. Backus. Ribbon like petals, of royal scarlet color; back of petals silvery rose ; fine.

George Maclure. Nine inches in diameter ; purple shaded amaranth ; outer petals tubular, inner ones broad, flat and incurved ; promises to be the largest of its class; was awarded three certificates.

G. F. Moseman. An improved bi-color, being a brighter color; bright crimson, tipped with golden yellow ; this has proved to be one of the finest of all the new ones.

Gertrude Henderson. Lemon yellow, with flat fringed petals; lasts a long time.

Golden John Salter. Golden yellow, changing to amber; incurved.

Golden Queen of England. Very large and rich lemon yellow ; one of the best ; incurved.

Golden Fringe. Bright gold ; most distinct.

Golden Empress of India. Same habit as Empress of India, but of a very handsome straw color.

Gold. As name denotes, this is of the clearest golden yellow, and is perfectly double ; one of the best new yellows.

Gold Band. Handsome compact flower, round yellow petals.

H. Waterer. Late yellow, reflexed petals.

Hiver Fleuri. Flowers large, much fringed and of good size; early and free; creamy white and blush.

Incomparable. Rich crome yellow and old gold, mottled with bronze; a fine early variety.

Isic Japanese. Pink and rose, very free.

Jno. Salter. Fine dark Chinese, round spherical blooms.

Jessica. Snowy white, with yellow centre; very large flowers.

Jennie Y. Murkland. Most distinct ; very large, having a flat surface from which project long tubular rays, rich golden yellow, shaded with apricot and rose; a superb variety.

Josephine. Beautiful bronze yellow ; free and good.

John Thorpe. Eight inches in diameter; full flowers with long broad petals, except the under row, which contains a few tubular ones; color richest deep lake, a new shade; very early and vigorous.

Judge Roa. A delicate shade of pink; flowers seven and a half inches in diameter; a profuse bloomer, but its best feature is its earliness.

John Collins. Immense, large, flat flowers of beautiful silvery bronze, and ashes-of-rose color; very pretty.

John Welch. Dark crimson maroon.

John H. Bradbury. Deep crimson, tipped with yellow; fine reflexed flowers, in style like Duchess.

John M. Hughes. Awarded first prize and extra silver medal by Pennsylvania Horticultural Society in 1886; in color a beautiful silvery pink

King of Crimsons. A good sized flower of the most intense rich crimson, and of handsome globular shape; this is an entirely new shade.

Lord Wolseley. A grand variety; rich, deep bronzy red, shaded purple; one of the very finest.

Lady Slade. Soft pink, with lilac shade; most beautiful shape; incurved.

Lady St. Clair. One of the most beautiful of all whites; incurved.

La Desire. Fine white Pompone.

La Contaure. Light pink, changing to white; fine.

Le Tonkin. Centre white, shaded rose on the outside; flowers large, produced in bouquets.

Lady Talfourd. Delicate rose, silvery back, incurved.

Lord Byron. Large orange, tipped with red.

La Chinoise. Deep crimson, finely twisted petals.

Lord Mayor. Carmine violet, white ground, shaded rose; dwarf and free; a profuse and fine bloomer, opening last week in September; one of the best for pot culture.

Lady Matheson. Large petals, reflexed at extremities; globular, and rosy cream color.

Le Cygne. Flowers extremely large and of the most beautiful form; long tube shaped petals, creamy white; one of the best for all purposes.

Le Chevrefeuille. Flowers large, petals spiral; honeysuckle color.

La Triomphante. Pale lilac; reflex of centre petals cream; very large and fine.

Lady Selborne. A very large pure white variety of the greatest merit and quite early in flowering; remarkable for its flakey and snowy-like whiteness.

Laciniata Rosea. Tender rose color, pointed gold; resembling very much the old Laciniata in effect.

L'Ehourifee. Deep mastic yellow, petals reflexed; a very beautiful color.

Larraine. Resembles Ben d'Or in shape, but of brighter color; the flowers are borne on long, stiff stems; very full and fine.

La Nymphe. Delicate peach color, shaded white.

Louis Barthere. Very brightest crimson red, with under petals of old gold; flowers flat and very free; one of the finest of this much desired color.

Marsa. Rose, centre white; very free, blooming in the form of a bouquet

Mrs. R. Brett. Orange yellow; petals twisted, forming a perfect ball.

Montgolfier. Dark amber, gold reflex.

Mrs. G. W. Childs. Bronze tipped, old gold, reverse shaded salmon; extra.

M. Norman Davis. Carmine rose, and dark lilac; early.

Mrs. R. S. Mason. Heavy petals, cup form, of light buff color.

M. Bruulees. Indian red, tipped with gold; incurved.

Mr. Gladstone. Deep chestnut red; incurved; fine shape.

Maud. Very bright pink flowers of medium size; flowers in clusters; very good for cut flowers.

Mrs. George Rundle. One of the most beautiful white in cultivation; incurved; a popular sort.

Mrs. Mary Morgan. Rich, deep pink; perfect shape; incurved.

Mrs. Littlejohn. Richest golden yellow, some flowers being marked with bright red; of medium size, prolific in bloom, and very effective.

Mabel Ward. Lemon yellow, shaded silvery pink on back of petals; flowers very large and globular; a truly beautiful variety.

Mons. Roux. Red chestnut; like Baron Beust, only larger; incurved.

Mrs. George Bullock. Pearly white, flowers very large and flat; very fine for exhibition purposes.

Mrs. N. Hallock. Compact Chinese of rosy pink shade.

Mad. Thibaut. Fine dark red; valuable as a late variety.

M. Tarin. Silvery pink, very free and desirable.

Mrs. J. B. Wilson. Resembling Mrs. F. Thompson; white and rose shading, changing to lavender; extra large blooms, and a first-class sort.

Mad. Boucharlar. Rich mahogany; vigorous and free bloomer.

Mrs. Wanamaker. Probably the most beautifully shaped pearly pink in cultivation.

Mrs. Frank Thomson. Large, incurved, with broad petals; mottled deep pink, with silvery back; very distinct; flowers eight in. across.

M. Planchenau. Mauve, shaded rose and silver; flowers large; free and early.

M. A. Vilmorin. Medium size flower; full centre of beautifully whorled petals; reflexed petals of crimson and old gold, distinctly marked with crimson beautifully twisted and undulating; very late.

M. E. Nichols. Salmon yellow; of medium size and in bouquets of four or five pretty flowers.

M. Norman Davis. Deep rose carmine, shaded lilac; large flowers; one of the best.

M. Freeman. A grand flower; silvery rose, shaded violet; very handsome.

M. Ghys. A very effective, much frized flower of satin pink, pointed with yellow; a fine variety.

M. John Laing. Richest crimson; of the largest size and very distinct and fine.

M. Boyer. Beautiful pink.

Mad. C. Audiguer. Flowers of the largest size, of the purest rosy pink; a gem.

Mad. de Sovin. Rosy amaranth, shaded with silver; a pleasing color; flowers large and fine.

Md'lle M. Fabre. Silvery pink, with white shadings; large and finely shaped; beautiful.

Mad. Lacroix. Flowers of a light rose, changing into pure white; this is a superb variety.

Mary Salter. A beautiful feathery flower of creamy white; large and fine.

Martha Harding. Yellow, shaded brown; large and full.

Minnie Miller. Dark rose; very free flowering; this may be described as the best rose colored.

Moonlight. Immense flowers of pure white; a white Temple of Solomon.

Mr. T. Norris. Rich velvety amaranth; a reflexed flower of most brilliant color; golden centre.

Mr. W. Barr. Entirely distinct; base of petals the brightest crimson, partly tubular, with points of pure yellow; early, lasting a long time.

Mrs. Cleveland. A pure white with long tubular petals.

Mrs. Vanaman. Cherry red; very large and perfectly distinct.

Mrs. C. H. Wheeler. Flowers are of the largest size, and of such heavy substance that they look as if stamped out of leather; color a bright crimson on the upper side of petals, while the under side is clear old gold, thus forming a most beautiful contrast.

Mrs. Frank Thomson. Large incurved Japanese with broad petals, lined and mottled deep pink, with silvery back; very distinct.

Mrs. John Thorpe. Brilliant crimson; very decided in coloring; petals tubular half their length, disposed in a very marked whorled shape.

Mrs. R. Brett. A distinct variety, differing from all other varieties in its peculiar plume like flower and rich coloring of pure gold; a gem.

Mrs. E. G. Gilmore. Silvery pink petals; very large, partially quilled, and incurved to the centre; this will make a fine exhibition variety.

Mrs. C. Carey. A magnificent variety, with very large, broad petals of pearly white, much curved and twisted; on first opening, the flowers show a disc, but afterwards the petals incurve and form a nearly perfect ball in shape.

Mrs. William Mencke. Brightest yellow, with slender petals of peculiar shape; late.

Mrs. Langtry. An enormous incurved Japanese; flowers one foot across, outer petals long and quilled, inside ones flat and most beautifully incurved; color pure white; charming.

Nathan E. Roist. Flower snow white, of enormous size, broad petals and golden yellow centre; good for cut flowers, as it is finely in appearance and very pure in color.

Newport. The largest and best of its class; clear rose pink, opening flat and forming with age; ribbon like balls of the largest size; a splendid variety; first-class certificate.

Nelly Bly. Brilliant yellow, large flowers, which are plumed and tasseled; a splendid variety.

Nuit d'Automone. Richest crimson amaranth, beautiful color; largest size.

Nut de Helver. Old gold and bronze, late.

Othello. Single bronze red color, free and good.

October Beauty. One of the earliest varieties, flowering by October 1st; medium size, good substance, lasting color, at first a dull pink changing to white.

Osiris. Rose, shaded lilac; globular shape.

Old Gold. A free blooming sort of a handsome old gold color.

President Hyde. Large, full double reflexed twisted outer florets; color, rich yellow; of fine habit and free flowering.

Prince Alfred. Rose crimson, shaded silvery purple; incurved; very fine.

Perle Precieuse. Purple, tinted silvery rose; broad petals, and perfectly incurved high centre; a valuable addition.

Public Ledger. Named after the Ledger newspaper; softest pearly pink; very large and so incurved as to resemble a ball.

Puritan. White, tinted with lilac; large, good habit, and one of the finest for bush plants.

Prince of Orange. Brilliant yellow, shaded and edged with a narrow band of red; very fine.

Pelican. The finest of recent introduction; pure white shaded cream petals, irregular, flat, half tubular.

Phœbus. This is without any exception one of the finest yellow ever grown; flowers large and handsome; too much could not be said of this variety.

President Garfield. Brightest carmine; large flowers and very distinct.

Pietro Diaz. Brilliant red, fine habit, large flowered.

President Arthur. Immense rose flowers, opening in whorls; was exhibited measuring seven inches across.

Purple King. Deep purple, rather late, but quite distinct in color.

Peter the Great. A most showy bright lemon yellow variety; beautiful foliage and fine habit.

President Spaulding. Very vigorous, of a rich reddish purple color.

Queen of Lilacs. Handsome Chinese variety; lilac.

Queen of England. Very large, fine blush; partially incurved.

Robert Crawford, Jr. A seedling of Mrs. Frank Thomson; color white, under petals slightly tinged; very choice and large.

Rob Roy. Orange, turning to gold; yellow centre and globular form.

Robert Bottomly. Pure white; large flowered; very fine.

Rose Lace. Flowers medium size, each petal toothed; dark rose; very pretty.

Rosenm Pictum. Very large, deep rose, silvery reflex; fine habit; distinct.

Snowdrift. Reflexed white flat petals, fimbriated; medium size; robust habit.

Salteri. Brilliant red, reflexed; neat and very beautiful flowers, having many petals; deep golden yellow.

Sir B. Seymour. Deep bronzy red on upper petals, finely incurved; light rosy shade on the outside.

Sœur Melanie. Flowers small, reflexed, of the snowiest white.

St. Patrick. Bronzy red, large, incurved; distinct.

Soleil Levant. Pale yellow; large quilled petals; a grand yellow.

Stars and Stripes. Streaked with pink and rose; free and good.

Sadie Martinot. Fine bright yellow; very late.

Source d'Or. (Golden Stream.) Golden twisted florets, tipped yellowish brown; very large flowers.

Syringa. Lilac; of immense size, centre petal increasing, other petals very irregular.

Thunberg. Flowers very large, petals long and much incurved; a pure primrose shade of yellow.

Theodora. Rosy salmon with pale centre.

Tronbadour. Rosy pink; of fine form and large flowers.

Thomas Cartledge. A grand variety; pure orange color of great size.

Timbal d'Argent. An exquisite pure white Anemone flowered kind, the most admired of any in its class; it flowers with the greatest profusion.

Tubiflorum. Tubular shaped petals, odd and interesting.

Telfour Salter. Rich, deep crimson, of large size, forming dense heads of flowers, pointed with yellow.

Tragedie. Rather small, of a new shade of color, rose, pink, and blush; a neat, pretty flower.

Venus. Lilac peach; large and beautiful, incurved.

Vallede Andore. Maroon, yellow shaded, petals twisted.

Webb's Queen. A late bloomer; rich silvery rose; perfect bloomer.

Wm. Joyce. Single, rosy pink; very free and fine.

Winonah. This was shown as Blushing Beauty and indeed is a beauty; the base of the petals is pure white, laced with deep lavender pink; flowers of the largest size, full and double.

W. M. Singerly. A beautiful shade of lilac; flowers large; strong grower and bloomer; promises to be very popular.

W. A. Harris. Nankeen yellow balls, with red centre.

COLLECTIONS FOR SPECIAL PURPOSES.

The following lists are selected with much care, and will be found very suitable for the purposes named. A wide experience, and knowledge of all varieties in current cultivation, guarantees the propriety of this claim.

FORTY-EIGHT OF THE BEST VARIETIES FOR SPECIMEN PLANTS OR GARDEN DECORATION. Price $5.00.

Cullingfordll	Red.	Lord Mayor	Violet.
Mad. C. Audiguier	Pink.	Lambeth	White.
Mrs. Frank Thomson	Pink.	Louis Weile	Mauve.
Domination	White.	R. Bottomley	White.
Duchess	Red.	Venus	Blush.
Le Tonkin	Pink.	Wm. Robinson	Golden Bronze.
Lord Byron	Bronze.	Wm. M. Singerly	Purple.
Mrs. Bullock	White.	Leopard	Spotted.
Mrs. Heale	Blush White.	W. W. Coles	Red.
Montplaisant	Crimson.	Troubadour	Pink.
M. Boyer	Pink.	Nymphea	White.
October Beauty	Blush.	Lucretia	Cream.
Puritan	Blush.	Mrs. Carnagie	Red.
Pellean	White.	Lilian B. Bird	Pink.
Mrs. R. Elliott	Yellow.	Empress of India	White.
Grandiflorum	Yellow.	L'Canning	White.
John Thorpe	Amaranth.	Mrs. Langtry	White.
Jean d'Arc	Blush.	Mrs. Vannaman	Red.
Gloriosum	Yellow.	Mrs. J. C. Price	Yellow.
Mrs. J. Wanamaker	Lilac.	Lady Matheson	Cream White.
Gold	Yellow.	Little Lycoon	Rose.
R. Crawford, Jr	Pink.	Ben d'Or	Yellow.
Peter the Great	Yellow.	Judge Rea	Pink.
La Triomphante	Rose.	The Bride	White.

FORTY-EIGHT OF THE BEST JAPANESE VARIETIES, SUITABLE FOR EXHIBITION FLOWERS. Price $5.00.

Baronne de Prailly	Pink.	Phœbus	Yellow.
J. Delaux	Crimson.	Pelican	White.
Boule d'Or	Yellow.	Public Ledger	Pearl Pink.
Comte de Germiny	Bronze.	Pres. Arthur	Pink.
Mrs. C. H. Wheeler	Orange Red.	R. Broklebank	Yellow.
Mad. C. Audiguier	Pink.	R. Crawford, Jr	Pink.
Domination	White.	Syringa	Peach.
Mrs. Frank Thomson	Pink.	Thos. Cartledge	Buff.
G. F. Moseman	Terra Cotta.	Charles Pratt	Claret.
George Maclure	Amaranth.	Soliel Levant	Yellow.
Grandiflorum	Yellow.	Lady Lawrence	White.
Gloriosum	Yellow.	Troubador	Pink.
John Thorpe	Amaranth.	Mrs. T. H. Spaulding	White.
Mrs. J. N. Gerard	Pink.	W. W. Coles	Red.
Mrs. A. Waterer	White.	Wm. Robinson	Golden Bronze.
J. Mahood	Yellow.	H. Cannell	Yellow.
La Triomphante	Rose.	Mrs. Carnagie	Red.
Le Dauphinois	Chrome.	Mrs. A. Hardy	White.
Mrs. Langtry	White.	L. B. Bird	Pink.
Le Tonkin	Pink.	Pres. Spaulding	Red.
Lord Byron	Bronze.	Little Tycoon	Rose.
Mrs. George Bullock	White.	Jessica	White.
Magnet	Pink.	Mrs. J. B. Wilson	Light.
Martha Harding	Old Gold.	The Bride	White.

TWENTY-FOUR OF THE BEST JAPANESE VARIETIES, SUITABLE FOR EXHIBITION BLOOMS. PRICE $2.25.

Comte de Germiny	Bronze.	Robert Bottomley	White.
Mrs. C. H. Wheeler	Orange Red.	Thomas Cartledge	Buff.
Domination	White.	J. Delaux	Crimson.
Mrs. Frank Thomson	Pink.	Wm. Robinson	Golden Bronze.
G. F. Moseman	Terra Cotta.	Soleil Levant	Yellow.
Grandiflorum	Yellow.	R. Brocklebank	Yellow.
La Triomphante	Rose.	The Bride	White.
Mrs. Langtry	White.	Mrs. Carnagie	Red.
Le Tonkin	Pink.	Pres. Spaulding	Red.
Lord Byron	Bronze.	Mrs. J. B. Wilson	White.
Phœbus	Yellow.	L. B. Bird	Pink.
Pres. Arthur	Pink.	Little Tycoon	Rose.

TWELVE OF THE BEST VARIETIES FOR BUSH PLANTS—SUITABLE FOR EXHIBITION OR CONSERVATORY DECORATION. Price $1.00.

Cullingfordll	Crimson.	Mrs. R. Elliott	Yellow.
Grandiflorum	Yellow.	Mrs. Langtry	White.
Mrs. J. Wanamaker	Lilac.	Nymphea	White.
Gold	Yellow.	Montgolfier	Bronze.
M. Boyer	Pink.	Mrs. Carnagie	Red.
Puritan	Blush.	Lady St. Clair	White.

TWENTY-FOUR OF THE BEST VARIETIES FOR BUSH PLANTS—SUITABLE FOR EXHIBITION OR HOME DECORATION. Price $2.00.

Cullingfordil..................Red.	Venus..........................Blush.
Grandiflorum................Yellow.	Wm. Robinson................Golden Bronze.
Jean d'Arc....................Blush.	Wm. M. Singerly.............Purple.
Mrs. J. Wanamaker.........Lilac.	Mrs. R. Elliott................Yellow.
Gold............................Yellow.	Mrs. A. Hardy................White.
R. Crawford, Jr.............Pink.	Mrs. Carnagie................Red.
Lord Byron...................Bronze.	The Bride.....................White.
Montphalsant................Crimson,	La Triomphante..............Pink.
M. Boyer......................Pink.	Empress of India.............White.
Puritan........................Blush.	Gloriosum.....................Yellow.
Mrs. Langtry..................White.	Mrs. Vanmaman..............Red.
Robert Bottomley............White.	Judge Rea.....................Pink.

TWELVE OF THE BEST JAPANESE VARIETIES SUITABLE FOR EXHIBITION BLOOMS. Price $1.25.

Comte de Germiny...........Bronze.	J. Delanx.....................Crimson.
E. Molyneux..................Crimson.	Robert Bottomley............White.
G. F. Moseman...............Terra Cotta.	The Bride.....................White.
Grandiflorum.................Yellow.	Mrs. J. H. Wilson............White.
Mrs. Langtry.................White.	Mrs. Carnaige................Red.
Phoebus......................Yellow.	Pres. Arthur..................Pink.

TWELVE OF THE BEST VARIETIES SUITABLE FOR GROWING AS STANDARDS. Price $1.00.

Comte de Germiny...........Bronze.	Grandiflorum..................Yellow.
Duchess........................Red.	R. Crawford, Jr...............Pink.
Mrs. Frank Thomson.........Pink.	R. Bottomley..................White.
G. F. Moseman................Terra Cotta.	Mrs. J. B. Wilson.............White.
Gold............................Yellow.	Mrs. Carnagie.................Red.
Jean d'Arc.....................Blush.	Mrs. C. Audiguer............Pink.

OUR PRIZES.

FORTY DOLLARS IN GOLD.

In order to further induce the higher cultivation of the Chrysanthemum in the South, we take pleasure in offering the above sum to the parties that raise the largest blooms. Full instructions are given in our article on Chrysanthemum culture of how to grow them. We have tried to be as explicit as possible, so that success must be certain to all who follow our rules. We have retained no trade secrets, but give it all away as far as we know. The prizes will be distributed as follows :

For the best 36 blooms, not less than 12 varieties, first prize, - - $25 00

For the 2nd best 36 blooms, not less than 12 varieties, second prize, 10 00

For the 3rd best 36 blooms, not less than 12 varieties, third prize, - 5 00

These blooms must be sent to us by express any time from the 1st to the 15th of November next. There will be no entrance fee for this contest, but no one is eligible to compete whose name does not appear on our order book this Spring for a sum of not less than THREE DOLLARS in Chrysanthemums. Any further information desired on this subject will cheerfully be given. In Fall Catalogue we will give full instructions as to how the flowers ought to be cut and shipped. The blooms eligible to compete for this must be of good size, only one bloom on each stem, and cut with a long stem.

CHRYSANTHEMUM CULTURE.

FEW plants will exist under as much neglect as a Chrysanthemum, and yet there is none more capable of being so highly developed than this now all popular plant. Out of the hundreds, probably thousands, of ladies and others that grow Chrysanthemums, only a very small proportion of them give them the proper treatment. In most cases after they set their plants out in the Spring, nothing further than a little working and weeding, and perchance a stake to keep them off the ground, is about the sum and total of the cultivation they receive. With such treatment as this you may get a very showy plant in the Fall that to a majority of people would appear very pretty, but good flowers or handsome plants can never be attained in this way. It is not many years since it was said that the Chrysanthemum would not do well in the South, but our experience and the experience of others at various points throughout the entire South have completely refuted all that has been said in that direction. We believe on the contrary that the climate of the South is especially suited to its cultivation, and we are determined to prove it not only by our own practice here, but by the care and cultivation our plants receive by all who follow our instructions, and as an inducement to do this we offer some valuable premiums to the parties that send us the finest blooms next November.

HOW IT IS DONE.

In early Spring secure nice healthy young plants in a fresh growing condition. Avoid those that are rather large and have a hard woody stem. These are plants that were rooted in November and December and got stunted through the Winter, and on this account will not make a vigorous growth, and are apt to rust and become unhealthy long before the Summer is over. Better far secure a nice growing plant with soft wood and in a healthy condition, if well rooted no matter how small, for it will soon grow off with much vigor, and if properly cared for, will retain it all the Summer and look rich and luxuriant when the large hard wooded plants before mentioned look stunted and less vigorous. We grow all our large specimen plants from cuttings rooted in February and March. We give elsewhere a list of the different varieties best suited for a special object of culture. After selecting your plants, choose a nice open spot where they will have sunshine each day. Make the soil rich to a depth of at least eighteen inches with cow manure, and a little bone dust if at hand. If the soil has a tendency to be stiff or clayey, add a little sand to keep it porous, as the Chrysanthemum delights in a rich rather light soil. Set the plants carefully out, taking care that the roots are moist and in no way suffering for want of water. As soon as your plants begin to grow, place a nice stake to each one. Allow only one shoot to grow, and when this has attained the height of about eighteen inches, nip the top off with the finger and thumb. Don't nip it down too far, just only the centre bud is all you want to remove. This will cause it to emit side branches, all of which must be removed from the lower part of the stem, and by no means let any come up from the roots. These

Mrs. Carnagie.

must be cut away as soon as they appear from the surface of the ground up to say about twelve inches of the main stem. No shoots must be allowed to come. All above this must be encouraged, and as they grow out must be nipped off at the end, as you did the main shoot, always having due regard for the shape and proportions of your plants. Through the early Summer months, when they are growing rapidly, this nipping will need attention every week or ten days, and by a close observation of these rules you will have a nice shaped plant on one stem to reward you for your attention. Be careful as the plant gets larger to add more stakes to keep it from breaking off at the joints, as Chrysanthemums grown in this way are very liable to snap off at the joints from the least cause. The neatest way is to put one strong stake in the centre and loop the different branches up to it, using a separate string for each shoot, and not pass the string entirely around the plant and tie it, as you would a sheaf of wheat, as is frequently done. This manner keeps the branches too close, and the air cannot circulate freely enough through them to induce their proper development. At all times during the Summer keep the ground around the plant nicely worked, never allowing the ground to become baked. Water

Mrs. Alpheus Hardy.

always in dry weather. This is best accomplished by making a little basin with soil around the stem of plant to prevent the water from running away when poured on, and cause it to soak in directly over the roots, where it will do the most good. In dry weather a little mulching of grass or litter of any kind thrown over the roots will prevent them from drying out so rapidly. After the first week in August all pinching and cutting must be discontinued, except any that comes from the roots or lower part of the stem; to allow these would spoil the appearance of the plant. Early in September the buds on many of the varieties will be beginning to form. At this time a watering of liquid manure should be given about twice a week, or say every alternate watering when the weather is such that watering is necessary. This is best made by placing about one-half a wheelbarrowful of cow manure in a barrel and filling up with water. Stir it up and let it rest for a few minutes before using. Water may be added occasionally, but the manure will last a couple of weeks. As soon as the buds commence to form they must be closely watched, and when about as large as peas, every bud but the one on the extreme top or end of the shoot must be removed. Just rub them off with the finger and thumb, and carefully preserve the end or terminal bud; this is where large flowers are required. It seems a great waste of the blooms to do this, but do it once and you will never regret it. One large flower attracts more attention in a display than a thousand small or medium sized ones. By this mode of treatment we had flowers that measured from eight to ten inches in diameter on a number of our plants that astonished all who saw them. It is best to cut away all the weak shoots and not let them flower at all. Select only the strongest shoots: leave only one bud on the end of each shoot; keep an eye on them occasionally, as little buds will keep coming lower down the shoot that must be removed. With this treatment, if large flowering varieties are selected, there will be no trouble in having blooms from seven to ten inches across, and a plant grown in this way with only a dozen blooms on it, is more showy and more attractive in every way than six of the best varieties you can secure grown, or rather let grow, in their own spontaneous way. During the period the buds are swelling give them plenty of liquid manure, but as soon as the blooms begin to expand, give them clear water. After the blooms are fully expanded, if shaded from bright sun they will last a much longer period. The culture in pots can be carried on exactly as the foregoing rules state; the same applies to both pot and open ground culture. When grown in pots they will have to be shifted into larger pots from time to time, as the growth of the plant demands it, and must be potted into the pots they are intended to bloom in not later than the first week

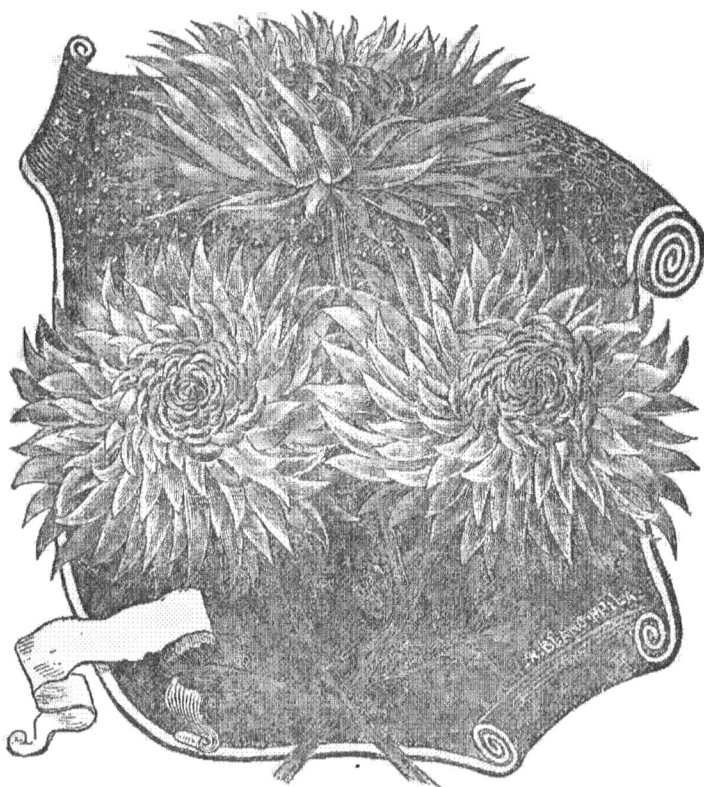

in July, and not afterwards disturbed at the roots. Keep the pots plunged or sunk in the ground up to the rim of the pot, as this keeps them from becoming dry so rapidly, and greatly adds to the health of the plant, as when grown in pots they are more liable to suffer from want of water, and consequently need more care than if they were planted in the open ground. When the plants are grown in the ground all the Summer and taken up and potted in the Fall for house or conservatory decoration, the transferring of them into pots is a critical period. This is best accomplished by the middle of September or October 1st, if the weather is cloudy and favorable. Plants intended for potting should be cut around from eight to ten inches from the stem with a sharp spade or knife, running the implement into the ground to a depth of about fourteen inches all around the plant; this cuts off all the rambling roots and induces the ones inside the circle to grow more dense and make a complete mass of roots, and if the above cutting is attended to about once a week for two or three weeks before potting, when the time comes to pot your plants will lift up with a nice ball of roots and suffer little or no check in the operation. After potting have a tub of water at hand and stand them in it for about twenty minutes, with the water above the top of the top. After this remove to the shade and keep them there a few days, gradually inuring them to the sun. If they show a tendency to wilt, keep in shade a few days longer, and keep the foliage moist by frequent sprinklings. Standard Chrysanthemums is the trade name for plants grown on a single stem to about the height of thirty or thirty-six inches, with a nice round head of bloom on pot. To grow them in this way needs more attention and skill than in any of the other ways. A proper selection of varieties best adapted for this purpose is of all importance, which we give elsewhere. The directions before given apply to these in same manner, only instead of nipping the top off at eighteen inches, the desired height of thirty or thirty-six inches,

as the case may be, must be attained before the top is pinched off. To attain
this height of the single stem, all side shoots must be carefully watched and
rubbed off as quick as they appear, also any shoots that show a tendency to
start from the roots, allowing only the one straight stem to grow, which must
have a good stake to protect it and keep it straight. When the desired height
is attained, pinch the top off and treat the new shoots that come from the sides
as before directed, and allow none to come out on main stem for say thirty
inches above the ground. If your main stem has not attained thirty-six inches
in height before pinching, of course shoots must be allowed to come out a little
lower down, so as to form a good head. In growing standards they must be
kept in pots all the time, that is where they are wanted for conservatory or
room decoration in the Fall, as there would be danger of loosing them when
transplanting to pots after all their growth was made in open ground. In the
far South, where they remain out all the time, it is not necessary to keep them
in pots, but may be grown to standards in the open ground with the same care
as the other Chrysanthemums.

RE is hardly a plant which is more popular among all
classes on the globe than what is generally known as the
Horse-Shoe, Zonale, or Fish Geranium. The Geranium
is found under many different circumstances; it helps to
embellish the conservatories of millionaires as well as the
homes of the humble and industrious, but it loses nothing
of its inherent beauty on that account. It wanders with
the household furniture from place to place, and the good
wife makes a special request to her husband not to forget
her Geranium. The propagation of the Geranium is universally known. Every woman knows how to slip it or
grow it from cuttings; it is also produced freely from seed. They stand the hot
sun of the South better than any other class of plants. They produce more
flowers and make a better display on whatever place they are grown than anything that could be grown on a similar space. Our stock is very fine, and much
larger than we ever sent out before.

An Extra Choice Assortment.

The following varieties are new and very beautiful. They attract attention wherever seen, by their rich and distinct colors.

Price 10 Cents Each, 14 for $1.00, by Mail. Our Selection, 16 for $1.00, by Express.

Euginier Clevoland. Single crimson, shaded purple; large.
Julius Lartigue Single rose; vigorous and free.
Tunisse. Double salmon; very handsome.
Countess Ettinger. Single violet carmine.
Francois Argo. Single peach and salmon tinted.
Leon Perrault. Finest single scarlet.
M. Jasnine. Double pink.
La Cid. Fine double crimson.
M. Press. Beautiful double salmon.
M. Carr. Double dark crimson.

Mrs. L. Durant. Single crimson; very free and good.
Mat Sandorph. Semi-double salmon.
Queen ef Belgians. Single white.
Gardner Gardett. Purplish crimson, single.
Louis Ulbach. Large single scarlet.
George Pardins. Double violet crimson.
Alphonse Daundet. Fine rosy salmon; very attractive.
Annie Gaubon. Double rose.
Kate Schultz. Finest salmon pink; a beauty.
Walter Scott. Rich dark crimson.

Double Flowering Varieties.

Price 10 Cents Each. Our Selection of Varieties, by Express. 20 for $1.00; by Mail, 16 for $1.00.

We have a number of fine well established plants in three and four-inch pots at 20 cents each; $1.75 per dozen.

Aimee Goubin. Violet crimson, scarlet shading, very large individual florets, of superb form.
Asa Gray. A light salmon dwarf; very free flowering.
Amolla Baltet. Best double pure white.
Admiration. Rose colored flowers; very large.
Bac-olnh. Immense trusses of large florets, centre beautiful salmon, petals bordered with lively red.
Belle N'nol?nno. Plant dwarf and floriferous, with trusses of large, full florets of a fresh and very attractive color.
Bruant. A grand sort; trusses and pipe of immense size, semi-double, color beautiful, brilliant and sparkling vermillion.
Bishop Wood. Scarlet, shading to vermillion.
Bridal Bouquet. Beautiful double white flowers, producing freely.
Blanc Parfait. Large round petals, perfect formed florets, plant dwarf and free blooming; a most beautiful variety.
Bauquise. Very large trusses of beautifully formed flowers, on strong foot stalks; color pure white.

Centaur. Carries the largest and most perfect truss of any of the pink doubles.
Candidissima. A large, full, finely formed flower of the most snowy whiteness, not changing to pink.
Charles Darwin. Rich deep violet solferino; the base of the upper petal marked with red; a vigorous grower and free bloomer.
Cesare Gandola. Flowers very full of peculiar yellowish-red color.
Conseller Galy. Large trusses of a clear, brilliant current-red color.
De brazza. Plant of free growing and blooming habit; very large trusses of large semi-double florets; color a beautiful madder orange.
Deputy Lafizo. A rich vermillion purple; extra.
Deputy Varnay. Rich pink base of petals; white.
De Torry. Beautiful shell pink.
Earnest Lauth. Color deep violet; extra large truss.
Ethel Beal. A rich pink shaded carmine.
Emily Lemoine. Rosy salmon.

A BLANC

Etoile des Roses. Color bright, beautiful china rose, base of petals pure white, truss extra large and finely formed.

Gloire de France. Large round flowers; color salmon white.

Gertrude. Color bright salmon, with centre and outer edges touched with white.

General Commerzienrath Single. Plant very free grower and of fine habit; color fiery madder, large round flowers.

Grand Chancellor Faidherbe. A new sort, very thick and double flowers, of a dark soft red, tinted with scarlet and heavily shaded with maroon.

Gilded Gold. Bright orange scarlet of flame color; flowers large, of fine form, branching habit; a very constant bloomer, and one of the best.

General Millot. Very large florets, trusses full, of immense size; color the same as that splendid old variety, Grand Chancellor Faidherbe.

Gustave Wideman. Plant of short jointed and free blooming habit; strong trusses of very large florets of a lively apricot color.

Gil Bias. Compact trusses borne on strong foot stalks; plant very floriferous and of finest habit; color currant red, striped fiery red.

Granitum. Reddish salmon, a beautiful new variety; distinct.

General Gordon. New; beautiful bright double scarlet.

Harriet Thorp. Delicate plush, shaded with pearl, pink trusses, large and well shaped.

Henry Cannet. Deep scarlet; flowers and truss both large; a first-class bedder.

Jewel. A velvety scarlet; one of the very finest.

Le Sid. Very compact, but vigorous in growth and of perfect habit; color brilliant crimson red.

La Prophete. One of the most magnificent double scarlets ever grown.

L'Anne Terrible. A blazing scarlet.

La Constitution. A glowing yellowish salmon, the nearest approach to yellow of any.

Le Negro. A rich maroon, the darkest variety we have seen.

Leontus. A rosy pink; large flowers and truss.

La Fraicheur. Plant short jointed and of very free growth, freely producing very large trusses of well formed flowers of a tender lilac rose; a new shade of color and quite distinct.

L'Eprouve. Semi-double flowers of a clear carmine, changing to dark carmine, base of petals a pure white; plant short jointed and free blooming.

Lolita Pena. Long peduncles; very large and semi-double flowers, of a lively magenta color.

La Victoire. Trusses large, flowers full and of fine form; color pure and constant white.

La Traviata. Very large florets and trusses which are freely produced, carmine violet, upper petals marked with fiery red.

La Vienne. Plant dwarf and short jointed, creamy white, semi-double.

L'Andalouse. Large trusses of pure white and beautiful flowers, which are freely produced; a plant of very free growth and of fine habit.

Marvel. Dark crimson maroon, an extra fine variety.

Mrs. E. G. Hill. Ground color pale blush, overlaid with a delicate lavender shade.

Mrs. Hayes. Very double flowers of a beautiful light shade of pink or flesh color.

Medora. A beautiful scarlet, shaded amaranth.

Mrs Charles Pease. A beautiful, distinct variety of a deep pink color, the upper petals marked white; a great acquisition.

Mon. Gelein Lovagie. The brightest orange shaded.

Mad. Thibaud. A beautiful rich rose, shaded with carmine violet.

Mad. P. Overin. A beautiful rich magenta; semi-double.

Meteor. Pink, shaded crimson; of a rosette form.

Mrs. W. P. Simmons. Flowers and trusses large, deep salmon with deep bronze shadings; plant of free blooming habit.

Marquise de Oysonville. Very compact trusses of the richest carmine Chinese varnish color.

Mon. W. Bealby. Red garnet reflecting to violet color; plant of good habit.

Mon. Jules Aldebert. Flowers semi-double, of a beautiful flaming capucine orange color.

M. Roche Alix. Large flowers, the lower petals a rosy salmon, centre and upper petals fiery salmon; distinct and beautiful.

Mad. Ed. Andre. Large umbels, full and well formed florets, color salmon with bronze shadings.

M. Hardy. Large flowers, a deep lilac and tender rose.

Mad. Hoste. Perfectly formed trusses of enormous size; florets very large and nicely formed; color a novel shade of tender salmon, bordered with pure white.

M. Henri Truchet. We have an improved L'Eprouve in this variety; color clear carmine, base of petals pure white; a splendid variety.

Mon. Derard. Light rose.
Mon. J. Oretien. Enormous trusses of a fiery red velvet color.
Mad. L. de Bourogard. Enormous trusses of very large double florets of the finest form; color a lively salmon, each petal distinctly bordered with pure white.
Naomi. Blush pink shaded white, a lovely color; one of the best.
Orange Perfection. Enormous trusses of orange vermillion colored flowers.
Palmyra. Immense sized trusses of well formed florets; color white; a fine bedder.
Panama. Enormous trusses borne on strong foot stalks; flowers full and well formed; centre of petals salmon vermillion, bordered with rosy salmon.
Prokup Daubek. Very bright, soft rose color, a most charming shade; a very beautiful flower.
Peter Henderson. A very fine variety with bright orange scarlet flowers of fine shape.
President Leon Simon. Flowers large and of perfect form; bright clear red shaded salmon; truss very fine and large.

Peach Blossom. Semi-double; beautiful rosy peach color; a good bloomer.
Phallas. A rich apricot orange, most vivid in coloring; trusses very large, habit neat and free.
Phyllos. Salmon centre; the edge of petals lighter.
Robert George. Deep crimson scarlet of great size; a free bloomer.
Richard Brett. A peculiar orange color, the nearest approach to yellow; good bedder.
Solferino Red, with fine solferino shade.
S. S. Nutt. Rich crimson, dark trusses, massive and profuse.
Telephone. Double scarlet.
The Ghost. A waxy white; good form and substance; very desirable.
Thibaut et Keteleer. Flowers semi-double, salmon, bordered vermillion.
Venus. A creamy white; very large truss.
Wilfred. Double white; very fine.
Wagner. A fiery carmine; large flower and truss; a profuse bloomer.
Wonnesful. An immense truss of orange scarlet flowers; produces freely.

Single Flowered.

Arc-En-Ciel. The trusses of this variety exceed in size nearly all the single-flowered; color lake red, upper petals marked with orange scarlet.
Adalaine. Pure white, with salmon center; very fine.
Alino. A rich vermillion scarlet.
Appolino. Bright scarlet.
Arizema. Pure white, shaded with a delicate pink.
Aralia. A grand orange scarlet.
Aurofera. A fine orange scarlet.
Bridesmaid. A light pink, dotted with brighter pink.
Beauty of Clarksville. A large rosy scarlet, with white eye; one of the best bedding varieties.
Beauty of Kingsessing. White, salmon centre.
Bridal Beauty. A deep mauve.
Beauty of Annandale. Large, full and intense scarlet.
Cyclope. Trusses large; color white, shaded salmon, with an orange centre plainly distinguished from the white.
Cosmos. Immense perfect formed trusses; florets large and finely formed; color salmon, with orange, brighter towards the centre.
Chanfrau. Large scarlet; upper petals shaded.
Constellation. A dazzling scarlet, with white eye; a splendid bedding variety.
Colonel Holden. A very beautiful rosy crimson; a distinct color and free bloomer.
Desdemona. Scarlet, with rose shading.
Dragoon. A ceris scarlet; very large truss and flower.
Eva. White, with salmon centre.
Excelsior. Scarlet, shaded crimson.
Eugenia. Salmon; very free flowering; large truss.
Electrican. A beautiful shade of rosy salmon, a delicate and novel shade.
Fairy Queen. Salmon centre; outer edge of petals white.
Flanmetta. Large scarlet, shaded with rosy salmon.
Favourite. Florets large and fine, truss of immense size, color beautiful sherry scarlet; plant of good habit and free blooming.
General Grant. Scarlet; a good bedder.
George W. Earl. Pure white, with broad, deep pink centre; beautiful large flowers; a free bloomer.
Girardin. Produces immense trusses; a clear rose color.
Henry Irving. Very large perfectly formed flowers of brilliant vermillion scarlet, with pure white eye; trusses of very large size on stout footstalks; plant of neat and compact habit.

General Sheridan. Brilliant crimson; of dwarf habit; large truss.
Heloranthe. Light gold dust red; cup shaped flowers; extra.
Harry King. A magnificent Zonale; a vivid crimson scarlet; extra.
Hilda. Pale rose, white centre; a delicate shade.
Jules Ferry. Splendid trusses on long rigid footstalks, which are held well above the foliage; scarlet red.
Jumbo Florets and trusses of immense size, of a rich deep crimson color.
Jean Sisley. The richest scarlet.
James Vick. Flowers and trusses of a great color, a deep flesh, with dark bronze shadings; of free habit.
Louis Uhlbach. Intense dazzling scarlet.
Lady Byron. One of the finest pink flowers with white eye.
Mrs. E. T. Keim. Pearly white with vermillion centre; large white eye.
Miss Blanche. Deep purplish pink, trusses of immense size and freely produced; this is a grand bedding sort.
Margnerete. An exceedingly beautiful shade of crimson scarlet, the upper petals of a lighter shade; one of the most distinct varieties.
Mary E. Foote. One of the most beautiful salmon colored, even shade; very fine.
Mrs. Hamilton. Rosy pink with a fine violet shade.
Minerva. A bright, rosy salmon; very large truss and flowers; a most beautiful shade; very free flowering.
Magenta. A crimson scarlet, shaded magenta.
Miss B. Garland. A rosy salmon, with pink shading; a new and distinct color.
Marshal Vaillant. Immense truss; extra large flowers; color rosy salmon; distinct.
Mrs. James Vick. White edges; pinkish centre. It is without an equal for Winter.
Mrs. Moore. Pure white, with a beautiful ring of bright salmon around a small white eye; of a dwarf habit; free flowering; very desirable.
Master Christine. Pink; a good bedder.
Mme. Edwin Bellott. A rosy salmon with a light shade; extra.
Mark Twain. Salmon, shaded rose and violet.
Mrs. Witty. A pink nosegay.
New Life. A sport from striped Vesuvius, having its bright scarlet flowers striped and flaked with salmon and white.
Nove. Plant vigorous and of splendid habit; large trusses of the purest white.
Poet National. Round florets nicely displayed; color of Baroness Rothschild rose, deepening to soft rosy peach.

Pauline Lucca. Pure white, large flowers; the finest of its color.

Queen of the West. Bright orange scarlet; very large truss; profuse bloomer; we know of no finer for planting out in beds.

Ralph. A fine dark crimson, suffused with amaranth; a large, well formed truss; very distinct; extra.

Rev. W. Atkinson. A fine dark crimson scarlet; very large flower and truss.

Renomie. Salmon, shaded with carmine; very fine.

Ruby. A very large dark scarlet, with immense truss.

Rosalind. Bright scarlet, shaded with rose; large flower and truss; one of the handsomest new varieties.

Rosetta. A large reddish salmon, center of lower petals white, upper petals a deeper shade; very free blooming.

Rembrandt. Upper petals rich velvety crimson, the lower petals being deeply shaded with rich violet.

Reflector. Very bright and handsome scarlet, with large pure white eye; trusses large and freely produced.

Rosy Morn. Beautiful well formed and bright rosy carmine flowers; of a neat, compact habit.

Renan. Exceedingly free flowering, trusses large, fine pot plant; bright salmon apricot with bright shadings.

Rosemond. A vermillion scarlet, beautifully shaded with rose.

Swanley Gem. An English variety of exceptional merit; color rosy salmon red, with large white eye.

Sam Sloan. A fine bedding variety; color deep velvety crimson, large truss and very free flowering.

Starlight. Pure white with broad pink centre and distinct pure white eye.

Sanguinea. A beautiful crimson scarlet.

Saturn. A very bright scarlet.

Sparkler. A bright crimson magenta; extra large truss.

Senator. A dark scarlet; very large truss.

Skeen Rival. A rosy scarlet; beautiful stems; zone creamy white.

Triumph. Rosy salmon, shaded pink; very large flower and truss; distinct and floriferous.

Victor Hugo. Plant dwarf and floriferous, trusses large, flowers fine form and finish, a brilliant salmon.

Voltairo. A large crimson scarlet; truss very effective.

Wood Nymph. Light pink; very free blooming variety.

Wm. Cullen Bryant. The finest shaped single flowering Geranium known; color a soft, rich, pure scarlet.

White Swan. A large bold white flower; fine for bedding.

Ivy Leaved.

Bijou. Hybrid; double scarlet.

Dolly Varden. Gold and bronze.

Gorman or Parlor Ivy.

Remarkable. Flowers rose and white; strong growing variety, suitable for hanging baskets. 15 cents each.

Gold, Bronze and Silver Leaved.

Bijou. Flowers a dazzling scarlet; leaves bordering white.

Black Douglass. Yellow, with dark zone.

Batterson Park Gem. Yellow and green.

Golden Harry Tricolor. Golden yellow, bronze zone.

Marshal McMahon. Yellow ground, with a bronze zone.

Mountain of Snow. Flowers bright scarlet, the leaves margined white.

Happy Thought. Entirely distinct from any other variegated Geranoum; centre of the leaf creamy yellow, with a broad margin of deep green.

Mad. Solleroi. New Silver Geranium; this is the greatest acquisition in variegated Geraniums, for bedding purposes, that has been introduced since the old Mountain of Snow.

Scented.

Apple. 25 cents each.

Lemon. 10 cents each.

Nutmeg. 10 cents each.

Oak Leaf. 10 cents each.

Pennyroyal. 10 cents each.

Rose. Three varieties. 10 cents each.

Mrs. Taylor. A distinct new variety of the rose scented Geranium, having large scarlet flowers. 15 cents each.

Pelargoniums.

These are more commonly known as Lady Washington Geraniums. The flowers are large, with deep blotches on the upper petals, and bright spots on the lower. While in bloom during the months of May and June, they are very beautiful and ornamental, either as pot plants or in the garden. Although their time of blooming is short, their great beauty while in flower makes them very desirable. 25 cents each.

Beauty of Oxton. Maroon, blotched crimson and white.

Evening Star. Salmon scarlet; base of petals white.

Empress of India. White, streaked crimson.

Emperor. White, maroon blotch.

Favorite. Delicate pink; dark blotch.

L'Avenir. Beautifully striped white and crimson.

Mrs. Bradshaw. White, blotched crimson maroon.

Mermeris. Rosy carmine; light centre.

Scarlet Gem. Scarlet crimson.

Rob Roy. Rosy purple; white eye.

The Belle. White, maroon blotch, shading to crimson.

General Taylor. Carmine, with crimson blotch.

DAHLIAS.

ANY think the Dahlia is the grandest Autumn flower we have. Nothing is its equal in any respect in September and October. It is in its glory when everything else is fading, and surrenders only to the Frost King. The Dahlia is divided into four pretty distinct classes, the ordinary or Show Dahlia; the Dwarf or Bedding Dahlia, the Pompone or Bouquet, with small, very perfect flowers, and the Single Dahlia, which is now becoming very popular, and especially desirable for cutting. As the Dahlia is a Fall flower, there is no need of planting before about the middle of May, or even later.

Price for Strong Tubers 15 Cents Each, $1.50 Per Dozen.

Young green plants, ready April 1st, 10 cents each, $1.00 per dozen. The tubers or roots cannot be sent by mail.

Show Flowers.

Alderman. Light shaded purple.
Adonis. New; yellow, amber, tipped; very fine.
Anna Neville. Pure white; extra.
Alexander Drammond. Shaded maroon.
Amazon. Yellow, with scarlet edge.
Ada Tiffin. Light peach; splendid form.
Aristides. Deep purple.

Burgundy. Rich shaded puce; very large.
Belle de Baum. Deep pink.
Bob Ridley. Bright red; splendid form.
Cremorne. Yellow, tipped red.
Canary. Pale yellow; fine outline.
Cochineal. Crimson, toned with a brownish shade.
Constance. Flowers are of the purest white and good shaped.
Duke of Wellington. Purple; very large.
Duke of Roxburgh. Salmon buff; extra.
Earl of Shaftsbury. Rich purple; exquisite.
Earl of Radnor. Deep crimson.
Earl of Peaconsfield. Rich plum; finest form and outline.

Emily. Light purple; very fine.
Edward Purchase. Beautiful bright crimson.
Estella. Cream white.
Fire King. Fiery crimson scarlet.
Flamingo. Deep vermillion scarlet.
Fraulein Hettergott. A dark maroon, tipped white.
George Goodall. Scarlet; most desirable.
Her Majesty. White, deeply edged with purple.
Hercules. Yellow, striped red; frequently self of a brownish red.
Henry Bond. Rosy lilac; large and fine.
Jennie Greive. White ground, edged with a rosy lilac.
Jourezl. Dazzling scarlet; long petals, curiously twisted at the points.
John McPherson. Rich violet purple.
John Sladden. Nearly black; extra.
John Harrison. Dark crimson.
John Kirby. Yellow buff; compact.
James Wilder. Rich velvet maroon, red shading.
James Crocker. Purple; fine.
King of Primroses. Primrose yellow.
Lady Mary Herbert. Yellow, tinted buff.
Lady Jane Ellis. Creamy white, tipped a purplish rose.
Lady Mary Wilde. White, tipped rosy purple.
Leah. Golden bronze.
Livonia. Lilac.
Mary Keyros. Fawn, ground edged a bright, rosy purple.
Mrs. Burgess. Purplish shading, occasionally white tipped.
Mrs. Stanton. Pure white ground, heavily laced with deep purple.
Mrs. Goodwin. Dark maroon; large.
Mrs. Standcomb. Canary yellow, very distinctly tipped with deep fawn.
Mrs. Piggott. Pure white; good form; fine.
Masterpiece. Rosy purple; large; finest form.
Mrs. Fordham. French white, tipped with soft purple.
Mrs. Gladstone. Pink.
Modesty. A beautiful shade of yellow, tinted pink.
Mrs. Hawkins. Rich sulphur yellow, light towards the tips.
Nemesis. White, shaded pink.
Netty Buckell. Light blush, tinted pink.
Oreole. Golden yellow; first-class.
Princess. White; large, full and fine.
Princess Alice. Light lilac; extra fine.
Paradiso. (William's.) Clear claret; new in color.
Paul of Paisley. The finest lilac.
Pearl. Pure white; dwarf.
Purity. Purest white; free and constant.
Rifleman. Crimson scarlet; constant.
Royally. Golden yellow, crimson tipped.
Rosette. Rose edged lilac.

Sir Joseph Paxton. Yellow, tipped with red.
Tom Green. Maroon, tipped white.
Tho Pet. Dark maroon, tipped with white.
Unique. Pure white.
Vesta. Purest white; very fine.

William Kynes. Orange; one of the finest formed flowers.
W. Fringle Laird. The finest maroon; large, beautifully formed.

Single Dahlias.

Ascalon. Rich purplish rose; a flat and well formed flower; very fine.
Albion. Rich, velvety scarlet; oval petals of heavy substance.
Canary. Deep canary yellow; free and attractive.
Cleopatra. A large, bright canary yellow.
Cicerone. A reddish scarlet; very large; most attractive variety.
Chrysus. A beautiful sulphur yellow.
Coccinea Lembriata. A beautiful fringed crimson scarlet flower.
Cervantesi. Very bright orange; a bold and beautiful flower.
Dr. Wright. A beautiful dark maroon, with purple shading.
Etna. A very large, crimson scarlet, star-shaped petals; one of the finest.
Francis Fell. A sparkling purple with a rosy hue; remarkably fine, extra.
Fusilier. White, changing to pink.
Fire King. Fiery scarlet.
Grenadier. A bright crimson.
Gracells Falva. Color crimson, beautifully serated.
Gracells Fulgens A brilliant crimson scarlet.
George Wyatt. Rich mulberry self; an excellent variety.
Heapastus. A grand orange scarlet.
Hesper. Purplish crimson; a very fine flat flower.
Irma. Fiery rose; very fine.
Kisber. Mulberry self.
Lothair. Delicate creamy white.

Lutea Lemblata. Large golden yellow disc; flowers of paler yellow; outer edges of petals fringed.
Lilicea. A beautiful light shade of lilac.
Lenoophylla. The best white.
Lutea. Yellow self; very free.
Lutea Grandiflora. Rich yellow; very large, well shaped flower; fine habit; extra.
Mrs. Langtry. Pale orange buff; vermillion centre.
Octoroon. A very dark maroon; large; an exceedingly free flowering variety.
Orange Phoenix. Rich orange self; very fine.
Othello. Canary yellow, tipped with reddish amber.
Prince of Orange. Beautiful orange color.
Primnlace. A beautiful primrose self.
Phoepas. Lilac tipped.
Paragon. Rich maroon, edged rosy purple.
Pentagon. Dark maroon self; very fine substance.
Rob Roy. An intense deep scarlet; a very fine and large flower.
Snow Wreath. Pure white; very free.
Stella Blanca. White; fine habit.
Scarlet Gem. Bright scarlet.
Single Zinnia. Rich crimson scarlet; a very fine flower.
Violet. Violet purple; fine habit.
Vivid. A bright crimson; scarlet petals; very telling flower.
Violace. A grand lilac.
Winnifred. A ruby red.

Bouquet or Pompone Dahlias.

The flowers of this beautiful class are small, suitable for bouquets, but as perfect in shape as any of the show varieties.

Burning Coal. Bright scarlet; fine.
Conflagration. Bright orange; tinted scarlet.
Coronet. Blush white, lilac tinted.
Diadem. Orange, edged with scarlet.
Firefly. Orange scarlet; fine.
Guiding Star. Pure white, imbricated as in Camellia Alba Fimbriata.
Gladiator. Rich crimson.

Glow Worm. A handsome yellow, tipped with cinnabar.
Little Bride. White; very small and free.
Little Beauty. Pure white.
Lo Nain. Crimson; very dwarf.
Our Tim. Buff, shading to peach.
Scarlet Gem. Bright scarlet.
King of the Dwarfs. Deep violet purple.

CARNATION PINKS.

HARDY CARNATION PINKS, next to Roses, are the most popular flowers grown. Young plants should be procured in April or May, and be sure that they are young plants, no matter how insignificant they may look, for large plants are ones that have been bloomed all Winter, and are comparatively worthless. Carnations are quite hardy, and should be planted as early as possible, just as soon as the ground is in condition to work. The soil should be quite rich, well manured with thoroughly rotted manure, or, if not to be had, bone dust may be used to a good advantage. To have a beautiful bed of Pinks in the Fall, the plants should be set out about eight inches apart each way; as the plants grow, they should be "stopped," that is, when the shoots of growth become six inches long, they should have the points pinched out. The operation should be continued until the 1st of July, when it must be discontinued if flowers are wished in August. Price 8½ cents each, 14 for $1.00, purchaser's selection. Our selection, by mail, 16 for $1.00; by express, 18 for $1.00.

Astoria Bortonii. Yellow, striped with carmine and white.

Buttercup. Magnificent yellow.

Clara Morris. Model flowers of good size; very pure white, with the edges of petals marked with crimson.

Charles J. Clark. A grand Carnation; pure white, fringed edge.

Ferdinand Mangold. This is the grandest dark Carnation ever seen; flowers large and perfectly formed; color brilliant red, shaded maroon.

Grace Farden. Flowers medium or large size and very freely produced; plant of grand habit and vigorous growth; a superb variety.

Inze's White. Good, strong, dwarf.

Inze's Red. Vigorous; very fine.

J. J Harrison. Flowers pure satiny white, marked and shaded with rosy pink; good size, perfect form, never bursts, and freely produced on long stems.

John McCulloch. This splendid new Carnation is the most brilliant and finest scarlet yet introduced.

La Purity. Deep carmine.

Lady Emma. Intense scarlet; a very profuse bloomer.

La Excellent. White, with carmine edge.

B. A. Elliott. This is the largest flowered Carnation in cultivation; vermillion scarlet.

Brussels. Cherry red, with broad stripes of carmine.

Lydia. Orange and rose; a very free and profuse bloomer.

Mrs. McKenzie. A very large pink.

Mrs. Carnagie. Color pure satiny white, with beautiful rosy pink stripes; flowers extra large.

Petunia. This resembles a double Petunia as to be most appropriately named; the flowers are large, of a lavender rose, mottled white and deeply fringed.

Portia. The most intense bright scarlet; the flowers of small size, but of fine shape and long stemmed, and freely produced.

Peerless. Pure white.

Peter Henderson. Pure white; very fine.

President Degraw. A very fine white.

Quaker City. Magnificent hardy white; very profitable for Spring forcing.

Sunrise. Orange, flaked with crimson; a new variety.

Snow White. Pure white.

Rawan. Dark metallic crimson maroon.

Snowdon. Free blooming; white.

OPYRIGHTED 1888

A. BLANC PHILA

VERBENAS.

We have a large stock of these useful and popular bedding plants, and grow them extensively. The following comprise the best and most distinct colors of the new Mammoth strain, the distinguishing peculiarity of which is that the flowers are very much larger than the ordinary type, each individual floret being of the size of a silver quarter dollar, and the truss fully nine inches in circumference; they are of all the shades known to Verbenas. Price 8½ cents each, 16 for $1.00, purchaser's selection. Our selection, by mail, 20 for $1.00; by express, 25 for $1.00.

Aurioula. Fine large purple.
Admiration. A rich clear vermilion; large white eye; extra.
Blue Bonnet. Rich deep blue.
Beauty of Oxford. Dark pink, immense size.
Bernloa. Crimson maroon; good flower.
Bijou. Rich dazzling scarlet, small white eye.
Blue Bird. Blush purple.
Oandidisslma. Finest white.
Columbia. White striped purple.
Century. Rich dazzling scarlet.
Coral. Fine coral pink.
Crystal. Pure white.
Damson. Rich purple mauve, clear white center.
Daisy Dale. Beautiful pink.
Endymion. Deep vermilion, crimson shaded, large white eye; extra.
Fanny. Violet rose, large white eye.
Flame. Bright dazzling red.

Glow Worm. Brilliant scarlet, perfect form.
Maltose. Lilac shaded blue.
Mrs. Massey. Salmon pink, large white center.
Marion. Mauve, perfect form, white center.
Miss Woodruff. Dazzling scarlet, very fine.
May Queen. Soft magenta pink.
Niobe. Deep vermilion; fine flower.
Nelly Park. Orange scarlet, splendid.
Purple Queen. Royal purp.e; large white eye.
Perfection. Rich chocolate maroon, lemon eye.
Rosy Morn. Pink, with large white eye.
Striata. White and purple streaks.
Sylpbe. The best white Verbena in cultivation.
Snow Flake. Pure white; large truss; a fine and healthy grower.
Scarlet King. A fine, vivid scarlet; dark eye.
Surprise. Clear, orange scarlet, with white eye.
Unaine. Clear cinnabar-red; extra.

CAMELLIA JAPONICA.

The rich and pleasing contrast afforded by their dark green leaves and their superb flowers of exquisite beauty and waxy texture, together with their almost endless variegations of color, combine to make them one of the most desirable of Winter flowering plants. Our collection comprises the following varieties. Price $1.00 each, nice bushy plants about sixteen inches high. We have no large size Camellias to offer this Spring.

Augustina Superba. Of transparent rose color, sometimes spotted with white.
Alba Plena. Large flower; white, imbricated.
Archduchesso Augusta. Beautiful red, with a dark azure vein and a white band in the middle of each petal, the flower assuming a blush and variegated color.
Angelo Cocchi. White, sometimes spotted or striped bright red, sometimes dark.
Archduchess Maria. Magnificent flower of good form, very double; vivid red, with white rib-bands.
Aspasia. Small petals, very compact, brilliant red, rosy white heart.
Auguste Delfosse. Fiery rose color, center of petals striped; finely imbricated.
Bella Romana. Flowers good; color soft blush, fluked with crimson.
Duchess de Berry. Flowers large, pure white; habit good, with fine foliage.
Fanny Bollis. Magnificent flower, well formed; large rounded petals of flesh white, stained blood red.
Imperatrice Maria Theresa. Large and splendid imbricated flower; petals bright red, changing to pure white.
Imbricata. Carmine red, sometimes of variegated color, hence called Imbricata Tricolor.
Jubilee. Extra large flower, imbricated; petals large and rounded; center white; lightly rose sprinkled.
Jeffersonii. Brilliant red, with narrow white lines across each petal.
Leon Leguay. Very double; red, shaded deep red, exterior petals undulated; a first-class variety.
Leopold I. Bright scarlet red, with plush crimson bars near the border of the petals; extra fine variety.
Lemicbost. Bright red, finely imbricated; a good variety.
Lyauna Superba. A vivid red, flower imbricated.
Matbotiana Alba. Pure white.
Madona. A grand flower; Ranunculus-like petals, sprinkled white and carmine striped.

Maria Theresa. Flower formed by eight or nine rows of petals, imbricated, very dense; white, with carmine red points.
Mistress Cope. White flower, crimson stripe; of splendid form; extra.
Bonomiana. Large petals, well rounded, imbricated in regular form; white line crossed through and through with deep red.
Chard·erl. Flowers large and petals broad, of a rich pink color.
Comtesse of Orkney. Pure white with carmine stripes, often peony form in the center, very large petals, sometimes a very bright red, shaded dark red or white rosy stripes, with the edges pure white.
Commendatore Betti. Superb variety, finely imbricated; red, changing to rose.
Comtesse Lavinia Magzi. Large buds; flower well formed, dotted cherry red.
Charlotte Papudof. Imbricated tricolor; the upper layers of the petals of rose color, sometimes of a pure white, with bright red border, interspersed with other petals of a beautiful rosy tint.
Candissina. Pure white; imbricated.
Madame Leboise. Imbricated, bright red.
Mathotiana. Deep crimson; large and fine.
Madame Ambroise Verschaffelt. Imbrication perfect; petals of medium size, very numerous, surrounded with a bright whitish color, veined and spotted rosy and red.
Noblissima. Pure white; peony formed; very highly valued on account of its early flowering.
Princoss Baclocbi. Superb flower, well imbricated; cherry red, with small white bands.
Prince Albert. Blush white, with numerous stripes of deep rose.
Princess Clotbke. Imbricated, nearly double; it has strong petals with large white bands and deep red bars.
Reine Marie Hourietta. Of very fine form, of splendid foliage; rose color, often speckled pure white; perfectly imbricated; very free bloomer.

Reine des Fleurs. Small leaves, but a vigorous grower, of good habit; a deep rich crimson color.
Trionfa di Lodi. Imbricated; large white petals, speckled and striped.
Tutonia Vorsicolor. Large flower; petals imbricated.

Triomph de Wondelghem. Flower red, central ribbon more bright, sometimes carmine with rosy white band.
Unica. Very large pure white flower, sometimes peony-formed; first-class variety.
Valtveareda. Very large flower of vivid red, often spotted pure white.

LILIES.

LILIES have long been celebrated for their chaste and rare beauty. It always has been and always will be a favorite. Its name has been handed down to us from the most remote ages, immortalized by painters and poets as emblematical of purity and beauty. No plants capable of being cultivated out of doors possesses so many charms; rich and varied in color, stately and handsome in habit, profuse in variety, and of delicious fragrance, they stand prominently out from all other hardy plants, and no herbaceous border, however select, should be without a few of its best sorts. During the months of February and March, we can send by express Lilium Harrissii, grown in pots, with stems from one to two feet high, fine healthy plants, for 50 cents each, that can be had in bloom at any desired time, according to the size of plants selected.

Lilium Auratum. Gold banded; the finest of all. 25 cents each; $2.50 per dozen.
Lilium Candidum. The white Lily. 15 cents each; $1.50 per dozen.
Lilium Davaricum. Red tinged, yellow spotted. 25 cents each; $2.50 per dozen.
Lilium Davaricum Incomparabilis. Spotted with crimson. 25 cents each; $2.50 per dozen.
Lilium Lancifolium Roseum. Blotched white and rose. 25 cents each; $2.50 per dozen.

Lilium Martagon. Purple. 25 cents each; $2.50 per dozen.
Lilium Longiflorum. Pure white. 25 cents each; $2.50 per dozen.
Lilium Harrissii. (Bermuda Easter Lily.) 25 cents each; $2.50 per dozen.
Calla Lily. Strong plants. 25 to 50 cents each.
Lily of the Valley. Strong clumps. 25 cents each.

HOW TO MAKE A LILY POND.

The best way to grow Lilies and other Aquatics for ornament, is to dig a place two feet deep and as large as you wish it, cement it, and divide it into compartments four by four (to keep them from spreading) by building walls one foot high across it with brick. Place good rich soil in this, and set one plant in each compartment. Set Bananas around the sides, and it will prove the greatest attraction you can grow, and well worth the labor bestowed upon it.

PLANTS FOR CARP PONDS, ETC.

All who are interested in the culture of the Carp know that the authorities on the subject make it a most essential point that the ponds should be stocked with abundance of Aquatic plants, for furnishing food, concealment, shade and the material upon which they prefer to deposit their eggs. We know from experience, that a pond well supplied with all sorts of plants will produce more than double the amount of fish than one without them. A pond stocked with these useful fish and with a collection of our choicest native Aquatics, together with the lovely tropical sorts, cannot fail to be an endless source of pleasure and profit.

WATER LILIES IN TUBS OR CEMENT BASINS.

For the open air a good degree of success may be attained by planting them in large tubs or half-barrels, on the surface or sunk in the ground. They should be placed where they will receive the full benefit of the sun for at least the greater portion of the day. Fill about half full with the soil recommended for Water Lilies. The next best arrangement for growing the Lily is to build of brick and cement a basin two feet deep and as long as you may desire, either round or square, with a convenient means for emptying the tank at the bottom.

Calla Lily.

Lilium Harrissii.

Nelumbium Specissum. It is the Sacred Lotus of India and China, and is also cultivated in Japan.

Nymphæa Oderata Rosea. This is the famous Red Water Lily of Boston; produces flowers larger than the white as commonly seen. It is very fragrant, and in every respect like Nymphæ Oderata, except in color, which is a deep pink shade, like Hermosa Rose. $2.00 each.

Sagittaria Variabilis. (The Arrow Head.) A native plant suitable for shallow water, growing about two feet high, bearing arrow shaped leaves and pearly white flowers. 25 cents each; $2.00 per dozen.

Nelumbium Letcum. There is scarcely any difference between this and Nelumbium Speclosum, except in the color of the flowers, which is of a rich sulphur yellow. A large patch of them, with hundreds of flowers and buds, is a sight never to be forgotten. Tubers, $1.00.

Nymphæa Odorata. Its lovely white flowers are worthy of a place beside the most costly exotics. It can be successfully grown in a tub and wintered in a cellar. Does well in one of the beds in the Lilly tank, but a more satisfactory way than either is to naturalize it in a pond, or slow running stream. Strong roots, 40 cents each, or three for $1.00.

Nymphæa Scutifolia. The Lilies cultivated under these names are of a beautiful shade of lavender blue, not a deep blue, about three or four inches across, but when the plant is given abundance of room and rich soil the flowers will be much larger, and of a decidedly deeper tint. They are very fragrant, the perfume being entirely distinct from that of Nymphæa Odorata. $1.00 each.

Pontederia Cordata. Another interesting plant for shallow water, with heart-shaped leaves and spikes of blue flowers, produced all Summer. 25 cents each; $2.00 per dozen.

CLEMATIS.

Of all the hardy running vines in cultivation, none is more beautiful than the Clematis, being entirely hardy and growing as they do more beautiful each year after being planted. They should be grown extensively. To anybody that has a position where a vine can grow, by all means, we say, plant a Clematis, for they are truly not only "things of beauty, but a joy forever." Small mailing roots, 50 cents each; large strong plants, 75 cents each.

Albertino. Double flowering; white.
Albert Victor. Lavender, with pale bar.
Amalia. Light bluish lilac.
Azurea Grandiflora. Azure lilac.
Excelsior. Violet purple.

Fair Rosamond. Blush white, red bar.
Gem. Deep lavender blue.
Gloire de St. Julien. White, yellow bar.
Hybrida Splendida. Reddish violet.
Helena. Pure white, colored anthers.

Imperatrioo Eugene. Pure red.
Jackmanni. Intense violet purple.
Jeanne de Arc. Grayish white.
John Gould Veitch. Rosette; lavender.
Lady Bovill. Grayish blue.
Lady Caroline Neville. French white.
Lady Londesborough. Gray, with pale bar.
Lanuginosa. Pale lavender.
Lanuginosa Candida. White tinted.
Lanuginosa Nivea. Pure white.
Lanuginosa Bellsairo. Laveuder.
Lavender Queen. Very strong: lavender.
Lawsoniana. Rose, purple veined.
Lord Londesborough. Mauve, red bar.
Louise. White, violet anthers.
Lucie Lemoine. White, yellow anthers.
Mad. Granger. Purplish red.
Mad. Van Houtte. French white.
Marie Lefebre. Pale lilac.
Magnifica. Reddish purple, red bars.
Mrs. Baker. Silver gray.
Miss Bateman. White, chocolate red anthers.
Monstrosa. Silvery white.
Otto Froebel. Grayish white.
Prince of Wales. Deep pucy yellow.
Rubella. Rich scarlet purple.
Rubre Violacea. Maroon purple.
Standishi. Light mauve.
Sophia. Lilac purple.
Sophia Flora Plena. Double flowering; lilac purple.
Star of India. Reddish plum, red bars.
The Queen. Fine mauve, Lanuginosa like.
Thomas Moore. Pucy violet.
Van Houtte. French white.
Virginia. Greenish white; fragrant.
Viticella. Dull rose.
Viticella Purpurœ. Bluish purple.
Viticella Rubra Grandiflora. Clear red.
Viticella Venosa. Reddish purple and veined.

AZALEAS.

ZALEAS are a class of plants highly ornamental for Winter and early Spring flowering; they are of easy culture and can be had in bloom from Christmas to May if a fair selection of varieties is kept up. Nothing can be more gorgeous than a fine display of Azaleas; their distinct and delicate shadings and pleasing graduations of color make them universal favorites, and they are now much sought after everywhere. We have now on hand one of the finest collections of these plants ever accumulated in the South, and take pleasure in offering them to our patrons, feeling sure they will yield them much pleasure and satisfaction. Our Azaleas will be this season, as usual, the very best for shape, variety and bud. Our general collection consists of the best market and show varieties. Plants are of perfect shape and short stems. Nice shaped plants, 50 cents each; large plants, $1.00 each.

A. Borsig. A very fine pure white and double variety, of good form and great substance.
Alba Illustrata. Flower of the purest white, occasionally sprinkled with lilac rose.
Alba Illustrata Plena. (Raphael.) Pure white, double, fine for forcing.
Alice. A splendid variety, with very double flowers of the most intense rose, with large vermillion blotch; it resembles its parent, Duc de Nassau, in growth and habit.
Apollon. Pure white, sometimes lined with bright red.

Amœna. Small semi-double flower, of a bright violet purple; a most profuse bloomer and an excellent forcing variety.
Baronne de Vriere. Flowers enormous, snow white, petals very large, with undulated margin, sparingly striped with crimson, and blotched with sulphur yellow.
Bernard Andrea. Rosy purple, double; very beautiful.
Bernard Andrea Alba. Superb white flower. very double; a most desirable and beautiful variety.

Ceres. White, blotched with rose; a very profuse bloomer.

Charles Enke. Rosy salmon, marginated with white; very fine

Charles Leirens. Semi-double, very dark salmon, large dark spot.

Charmer. Bright amaranth, the upper petals blotched with a deeper shade.

Cocarde Orange. Pure orange, with amaranth red spot.

Comte de Chambord. A salmony rose color, striped and edged by a wide festoon of the purest white.

Comtesse de Flandre. Clear rose.

Comtesse Eugenie de Kerchove. Semi-double, white, striped and spotted with a lively cherry; fine form.

Daphne. Fine large semi-double variety, pure white.

Dr. Moore. Intense rose, with white and violet reflection.

Deutche Perle. Double pure white; very free flowering and early blooming. If placed in a gentle heat it will flower at the beginning of December; it may be regarded as the best among the double-flowered whites.

Duc de Nassau. Dark rosy purple; a fine large showy flower.

Duchess Adelaide de Nassau. Fiery crimson, shaded with violet; a first-rate exhibition variety.

Etendard de Flandre. White, striped with purple.

Eugene Mazel. Rosy salmon, the upper lobes violet.

Ferdinand Kegeljan. Flowers of good form and substance, light orange salmon.

Fielder's White. Single white.

Flag of Truce. Pure white, double and very full; one of the finest double white Azaleas in cultivation.

Indica Alba. Single white.

Iveryana. White, with red stripes.

Jean Vervaena. Deep, rich crimson, edged with white, dark spot on upper petals; free flowering.

Juliette. Superb rose, beautifully feathered; fine form and good habit.

Le Flambeau. Glowing crimson, very bright and effective.

Louis Margotten. Large pure white, sometimes semi-double.

Mad. Dom. Vervaene. Vivid salmon rose, white margin.

Kenogin Cicopatra. Beautiful single variety, with exceedingly large flowers; white, spotted and striped with rosy carmine.

Mad. Camille Van Langenhoven. A snowy white, broadly banded with salmon and carmine, the exterior of the upper petals adorned with dark and yellowish green blotches; very fine.

Mad. Iris Lefebvre. Flowers extremely double, of a dark orange red, broadly banded and striped with deep brownish violet.

Mad. Paul de Schryver. The flowers are large, well made and very double, having the centre sometimes imbricated like that of a Camellia; lively violet rose.

Mad. Vander Cruyssen. Soft, glossy rose, tinted with amaranth; a very large semi-double flower; fine and showy.

Mad'le Loonl Van Boutte. A very fine white, flaked with rose and spotted with sulphur yellow.

Mad'le Marie Lafebre. A large flower of exquisite form and substance; pure white.

Mad'le Louise de Kerchove. A large, snow white festoon encircles the bright, flesh colored flowers, flaked with orange, blotched finely with maroon and shaded with carmine.

Mad'le Marie Van Boutte. Flowers very large, semi-double, white, flaked and blotched with rosy salmon; very fine.

Marquis of Lorne. The flowers are of a beautiful orange, with saffron yellow blotch; the petals are very large and round.

Model. Bright rose.

Narcissiflora. Earliest white variety, double; excellent for bouquets.

Oswald de Kerchove. A very beautiful variety of lake rose with fiery blotch; large and well formed.

President de Ghellinck de Walle. Very large double, of an intense rose, with very large lake blotch.

Princess Charlotte. Very large flower of a beautiful rose; fine form.

Princess Louise. Beautiful rose flower, with white margin and a large fiery carmine blotch.

Functulata. Creamy white, striped with vermillion and scarlet; spotted with very dark maroon; flowers very large.

Raphael. Alba Illustrata Plena. Pure white, double; fine for forcing.

Reine de Portugal. Good form and substance, flowers double and pure white.

Reine des Pays-Bas. Violet pink, margined with white and richly striped with deep crimson.

Reine des Roses. Beautiful bright rose, deeply spotted.

Roi Leopold. Rich glossy crimson; very fine form.

Sigismund Rucker. Flowers lilac rose, strongly netted and bordered with white, splendidly blotched with bright crimson.

Souv. du Prince Albert. Warm peach rose, deeply margined with pure white, double flower, prolific bloomer.

Superba. Bright rosy carmine, of good form; late.

Stella. Flowers large, fine substance and perfect form, bright orange scarlet, with rich violet upper segments, profusely spotted with lake.

Vittata Crispiflora. White, shaded with purple and crimson; very free and fine for forcing.

W. Wilson Saunders. A very fine white variety, striped and blotched with vivid red.

BEGONIAS.

This class of plants is each year becoming more deservedly popular. The beauty of their foliage and graceful flowers make them useful plants for greenhouse or window decoration. A number of new varieties of special merit are coming out each year. We would call special attention to Semperflorens

Semperflorens Gigantea Rosea.

Gigantea Rosea as a beautiful decorative plant; also Sutton's White Perfection, a handsome free flowering variety. Our stock of Begonia Rex is large this year, and contains some handsome and beautifully marked varieties. We will send by express twelve fine well grown plants of Begonias for $1.00, to consist of one Rex, one Semperfloren Gigantea Rosea, one Sutton's White Perfection, and one Metallica, the rest to consist of the other varieties named below, the selection to be left to us. This will make a fine assortment of this popular plant to begin with, and will well repay the outlay. We can send twelve smaller plants as above by mail for $1.00.

Alba Picta. A perfectly distinct variety. It is shrubby in habit, and of compact growth, having long, slender pointed leaves on short stems. The leaves are glossy green, thickly spotted with silver white, the spots graduating in size from the centre toward the margin; flowers white. 15 cents.

Begonia Rex. The Rex varieties, of which we have a dozen or more, varying in color and

markings, are very effective as pot plants; care should be taken to keep the foliage free from dust; occasionally the plants may be showered, but should not be exposed to the sun until the leaves are perfectly dry; a fine assortment. 25 cents.

Dregei. This variety is always in flower, Winter and Summer; it is one of the most useful plants we have; flowers are white. 15 cents.

Fuchsioides Alba. It has Fuchsia-like, pure white flowers. 10 cents.

Fuchsioides Rubra. Red flowers; a very fine and constant bloomer. 10 cents.

Nitida Alba. A strong grower and profuse blooming variety, producing immense panicles of pure white flowers; fragrant. 10 cents.

Parvifolia. A dwarf, bushy growing variety, with pure white flowers, being in bloom the whole year; a splendid sort. 10 cents.

Rubra. One of the finest Begonias in cultivation; its dark, glossy, green leaves, combined with its free flowering habit, make it one of the very best plants for house or conservatory decoration; the flowers are of a scarlet rose color, and are produced in the greatest profusion. 15 cents.

Richnifolia. Has large palmated leaves, supported on stems from three to four feet long. 10 cents.

Incarnata Metallica. Dark green leaves with silver dots and metallic shade; fine pink flower clusters. 10 cents.

Metallica.

Ingramii. One of the best Winter-flowering varieties; flowers reddish carmine, leaves edged with bronze. 10 cents.

Suttan's White Perfection. A beautiful dwarf, free flowering plant; always in bloom, and attracts attention wherever seen. 25 cents.

Semperflorens Gigantea Rosea. A superb variety, strong, upright growth, fine large flowers of a clear cardinal red, the bud only exceeded in beauty by the open flower, which is borne on a strong, thick stem; the leaves are smooth and glossy, and attached to the main stem; both leaf and stem quite upright growing, and forming a shrubby, round plant. 25 cents.

Saundersonii. Of this variety the flowers are a scarlet shade of crimson, borne in profusion during the entire Winter months. 10 cents.

Weltoniensis. A very handsome Winter flowering variety, giving in profusion its lovely pink flowers; of easy cultivation. 10 cents.

Zebrina. Erect in growth, of a beautiful variegated foliage, leaves shaped like that of Rubra, and bearing white flowers. 10 cents.

Glaucophylla Scandens. An early flowering and vigorous growing variety, producing its beautiful clusters of rich salmon-colored flowers from the axil of each leaf; its drooping habit makes it a very desirable plant for hanging baskets. 15 cents.

Hybrida Multiflora. Flower rose colored; it blooms almost continually. 10 cents.

Metallica. A shrubby variety; good grower and free bloomer; leaves triangular, longer than they are wide; under side of leaves and stem hairy; the surface of lustrous metallic or bronze color, veined darker; flowers white, covered with glandular red hairs; it is perfectly distinct. 15 cents.

FUCHSIAS.

These, when in full bloom, are the most graceful of all cultivated plants; nothing can surpass the beauty of well grown specimens. They delight in a light, rich soil, and may be grown either as pots plants or in a sheltered border. In either case they should be protected from the hot mid-day sun and from heavy currents of air. They require plenty of water and partial shade. Price 8¼ cents each, 14 for $1.00, purchaser's selection. Our selection, 16 for $1.00, by mail; by express, 18 for $1.00.

Admiral Courbet. Enormous double flowers; corolla deep violet, tube and sepals bright red.

Anna Maria. Long tube and sepals, double white corolla.

Admiral Mlot. Plant very bushy, free bloomer; large double corolla of a clear prune color, sepals brilliant red.

Alice Mary Pearson. Sepals creamy white, tube rather long, single corolla of a dark crimson red color.

Clio. Tube brilliant rose, sepals bright red, corolla single, purest white.

Col. Dominie. Of a very free branching habit, corolla very double and of an imbricated form, white striped rose, sepals reflexed and of a distinct, clear red.

Cleopatra. Very large and double corolla of an azure blue color, passing to dark violet; extra fine.

De Mirble. Plant of fine robust habit, sepals a bright red, large single corolla, violet and rose.

Elm City. Double purple corolla; one of the best; early flowering.

Earl of Beaconsfield. Bright red shaded orange.

Esmeralda. One of the grandest and most distinct varieties; tube short, sepals red, corolla very large and double, beautiful lilac changing to rose.

Flocon de Neige. Large bell shaped corolla of a creamy white, sepals clear carmine, plant dwarf, and of freest blooming habit.

Glory. Plant dwarf and busby, sepals nicely recurved, large single corolla, violet.

Harmonie. Plant dwarf and remarkably free blooming, very distinct in color, tender lilac shaded rose, sepals rosy white.

J. J. Rosseau. Very large and full corolla, a bluish violet, sepals bright red; in fact a very fine plant.

Joseph Rossin. Sepals red, corolla very large and double, dark purple striped rose.

Jeanne d'Arc. Sepals carmine red, corolla pure white.

Luster. Tube and sepals white, corolla scarlet.

Rose of Castile. Corolla violet, sepals white, of splendid habit.

Lamennais. One of the finest double white in the list; plant dwarf and hushy, corolla very large and double, of the purest white sepals, recurved carmine red.

Lady Heytesbury Improved. Single corolla, pink, early bloomer.

Mrs. Rundle. Single long red corolla.

M. Spuller. Plant of free blooming habit, the flowers semi-double, violet.

Milne Edwards. Very large double corolla, a dark purple.

Mazoppa. Very free bloomer, flowers single, sepals relieved, lively red, corolla violet red.

Annie Earle. Tube and sepals a waxy white, corolla single, clear carmine.

Berquia. Long flesh colored tube and sepals, corolla carmine.

Bulgarie. Large brilliant red sepals, extra large single corolla of perfect form, color a violet purple.

Coriolon. Tube and sepals carmine, corolla double, lavender.

Carl Halt. Corolla single, bright scarlet, with white stripes.

Mde. Von der Strauss. Flowers large, sepals slender and well reflexed, and of a pure red color; corolla white, large and double.

Mon. Thibaut. Plant vigorous and of remarkably free blooming habit, tube stout, sepals dark red, corolla rose vermillion, tinted violet.

Nellie. Tube and sepals creamy white, corolla single, flesh color heavily shaded mauve, early and fine.

Penelope. A grand single white variety, sometimes semi-double, corolla long and large, of beautiful form, and purest white, sepals lively red.

Parmentier. Sepals coral red, corolla violet, round and double.

Perle Von Brunn. Sepals recurved, very clear in color, of immense size, and has a double corolla of the purest white.

President F. Gunther. Corolla double, lilac and violet.

Phenomenal. This is, without a doubt, the largest purple Fuchsia yet produced, the flowers are twice the size of any variety heretofore introduced; corolla a purplish lilac, sepals a beautiful coral red.

Purple Prince. Double purple corolla; fine.

Raphael. Tube and sepals coral red, corolla large and double, very light blue marked rose.

Regent. Sepals recurved, a violet carmine, corolla double, violet and blue.

Snow Fairy. Double white corolla.
Storm King. The king of all the white Fuchsias; although it is claimed by some to have flowers as large as ten cups, we do not make such mistakes, but we say it is of a very large flowering variety, but of a very dwarf growth.
Speciosa. Pale red tube and sepals, dark red corolla; best Winter bloomer.
Surprise. Large single flowers, waxy white, corolla pale magenta bordered very dark.
Sen Berlet. Carmine tube and sepals, corolla of immense size, double, deep violet purple.
Victor Hugo. Very distinct, corolla lilac with rose stripes.

Saphir. Tube dark red, sepals long, a clear crimson, corolla single, blue, brightened with white at the centre of the petals.
Ville de Lyon. Lube large, sepals horizontal, crimson red, corolla large and double, white veined carmine.
Mrs. E. G. Hill. This magnificent variety was raised and introduced by M. Victor Lemoine, of France, and is undeniably the most perfect and beautiful double white Fuchsia ever raised; the short tube and sepals are a bright, rich reddish crimson color, corolla extra large, full and double, flower of the largest size.

PALMS.

The following is a select list of rare and handsome varieties, which can be recommended for apartments, conservatory decoration, or vase plants during the Summer. All are in a clean and thrifty condition suitable for making immediate effects, and require no nursing to bring them into proper shape. The Seaforthias, Arecas, Latanias and Kentias are of quick and graceful growth, and can be grown without much trouble.

Phœnix Spinosa.   Kentia Canterburyana.   Kentia Balmoreana.

Areca Baueri. A distinct and graceful Palm, excellent for table decoration. $1.50 to $2.00 each.
Areca Rubra. Foliage deep green, tinged red, stems red. 50 cents to $1.00 each.
Areca Lutescens. One of the most beautiful and valuable Palms in cultivation; bright glossy green foliage and rich golden yellow stems. 50 cents to $2.00 each.
Areca Sapida. A strong upright growing variety with dark green feathered foliage. $1.00 to $3.00 each.
Areca Verschaffeltii. One of the most elegant varieties, with dark shining green foliage and light-colored band through the centre of each leaf. $1.00 to $3.00 each.
Caryota Urens. An easily grown and useful sort. 50 cents to $1.00 each.
Chamedora Elegans. A pretty decorative variety with deep glaucous foliage. 50 cents to $1.00 each.
Chamærops Excelsa. A handsome Fan Palm, of rapid, easy culture. 50 cents to $1.00 each.
Curculigo Recurvata. A very graceful Palm like plant for decorative purposes. 50 cents to $3.00 each.
Cycas Revoluta. The stem of this variety is very thick, and bears the foliage in whorls at the top. $5.00 to $12.00 each.

Euterpe Edulis. Of spreading graceful habit. 50 cents to $1.00 each.
Kentia Balmoreana. A beautiful stong growing Palm, with deep green crisp foliage. $1.50 to $3.00 each.
Kentia Fosteriana. One of the finest of the Kentias, with graceful bright green foliage. $1.50 to $3.00 each.
Latania Borbonica. Chinese Fan Palm. The most desirable for general cultivation, especially adapted for centres of baskets, vases, jardinieres, etc. 50 cents, $1.90, $2.00, $3.00, $5.00 each.
Phœnix Reclinata. Beautiful reclinate foliage. 50 cents to $2.50 each.
Phœnix Rupicola. Of graceful arching habit. 50 cents to $2.50 each.
Phœnix Sylvestris. An attractive sort, deep green foliage. 50 cents to $2.00 each.
Seaforthia Elegans. One of the very best for ordinary purposes, of graceful habit, and rapid, easy growth. 50 cents each.
Pandanus Utilis. Screw Pine Called Screw Pine from the arrangement of the leaves on the stem. Excellent for the centre of vases and baskets, or grown as a single specimen; a beautiful plant. 30 to 75 cents each.

GENERAL COLLECTION OF PLANTS

SUITABLE FOR GREENHOUSE OR OUT-DOOR CULTURE.

ABUTILON—Fairy Bells.
Hard wooded greenhouse shrub, blooming almost the entire year; well adapted for house culture, and fine for bedding out in Summer. 15 cents.
Boule de Neige. A pure white bell-shaped flower, blooming without intermission.
Darwinii. Orange scarlet and pink veined flowers; blooms in clusters very freely.
Mesopotanicum. Trailing habit, bearing pendant flowers in great profusion.
Vexillarium Picta. Foliage small, mottled yellow and green; flower scarlet and yellow; of drooping habit.
Arthur Belsnam. Flowers large and of a dark crimson color.
Thompsoni Variegata. Leaves mottled with yellow.
Thompsoni Plena. This is a sport from Thompsoni Variegata; the foliage has retained the same variegation, but the flowers are perfectly double.
Golden Fleece. A bright yellow; very profuse bloomer.

Anthericum Variegatum.

ANTHERICUM VARIEGATUM.
A most striking novelty, introduced from the Cape of Good Hope. Very valuable as a decorative plant, being suitable either for the greenhouse, parlor, or dining table; the foliage is of a bright grassy green, beautifully striped and margined with a creamy white. 30 cents each.

ASPARAGUS TENUISSIMUS.
We cannot praise too highly this beautiful new plant. Its fine filmy foliage equals in delicate beauty the Maiden-Hair Ferns. First size, 50 cents; second size, 25 cents; small plants, 10 cents.

ACHRYANTHUS.
Any of the following are suitable to form ribbon lines in contrast with Centaureas, Cineraria, Candidissima, etc. 50 cents per dozen; $1.00 per 100.
Aurea Reticulata. Foliage beautifully reticulated with bright gold; stem of a very bright semi-transparent carmine.
Emersonii. Bright red, lance-leaved.
Lindenii. Rich dark red color, well adapted for either ribbon rows or the edging of flower beds.

AGAPANTHUS UMBELLATUS.
A noble plant belonging to the bulbous-rooted section, with evergreen foliage; the flower stalks grow nearly three feet high, crowned with a head of twenty or thirty blue flowers. 35 cents.

ASTERS.
Plants grown from choicest seed. 50 cents per dozen.

ALOYSIA CITRIODORA.
Lemon Verbena. A favorite garden plant, with delightfully fragrant foliage; fine for bouquets. 10 cents.

AGAVE—Century Plant.
Americana. Very picturesque plant for out-door decoration on the lawn, or growing in vases. 25 cents to $1.00 each.
Americana Variegata. Similar to the above variety, with leaves banded with yellow. These plants stand any amount of heat and drouth, and are therefore admirably adapted for center plant of vases, baskets, rock work, etc. Small plants, in four-inch pots, 25 to 50 cents; large, one or two feet high, $1.00 to $5.00.

Amaryllis.

AMARYLLIS.
The Amaryllis are an interesting class of bulbs, desirable for growing in pots, producing showy flowers that are very attractive and handsome.
Vittata. These magnificent varieties are vigorous in their growth, and produce a free supply of flowers, are flaked and striped with the most striking tints, and are justly esteemed the most beautiful of the Amaryllis family. 75 cents each.
Johnsoni. An elegant pot plant, with crimson flowers five inches in diameter; each petal striped with white. Flower-stalk two feet high, with clusters of three to five blooms. 75 cents each.

ASPIDISTRA LURIDA.
Curious plants, remarkable for producing their flowers under the surface of the earth;

the leaves are six inches long, about two inches wide, and of a bright green; they are well adapted for wardian cases, ferneries, etc. 50 cents.

Achania.

ACHANIA.
Malvaviscus. A greenhouse shrub, with fine scarlet flowers; blooms Summer and Winter; not subject to insects of any kind; one of the most satisfactory house plants ever grown. 25 cents.

Ageratum.

AGERATUM.
Very useful plants for bedding or borders, flowering continually during the Summer; by cutting back and potting in the Fall they will continue to flower in Winter. 50 cents per dozen; $4.00 per 100.
White Cap. By far the best and most useful variety ever sent out, being a dwarf, compact grower, and bearing profusions of pure white flowers; an exceedingly useful and profitable plant to grow for cut flowers in the Winter, as it blooms freely all Winter.
John Douglas. Azure blue; of very compact habit.
Meridan Gem. Compact; light blue.

ALYSSUM.
Double. A very beautiful variety, splendid for cut flowers; fine green foliage, and produces enormous quantities of double pure white, very fragrant flowers. 10 cents.

ALTHERNANTHERA.
Plants with beautiful variegated foliage, growing from twelve to twenty-four inches in diameter and six inches high; used principally for ribbon lines and borders. 5 cents each; 50 cents per dozen; $4.00 per 100.
Amabilis. Leaves tinted rose.
Aurea. Foliage dark green and golden yellow, the latter color predominating.
Aurea Nana. New; foliage bright green; beautifully variegated with yellow.
Latifolia. Broad, smooth, Autumn-tinted leaves.
Paronychioides Major. Bronze, tipped with red; the brightest and showiest.
Spatulata. Leaves tinted with carmine and green.

ACALYPHA.
Macafeana. A superb Summer bedding plant, with very highly colored bright red leaves; it prefers partial shade. 25 cents.

BELLIS PERENNIS—Daisies.
Well known ever blooming plants; pink, white and red; double flowering. 10 cents each; 50 cents per dozen.

BILBERGIA SPECIOSA.
Pineapple resembling foliage, with very bright crimson flowers growing out of the heart of the plant; of easy cultivation. 30 cents.

BOUVARDIAS.
These are among the most important plants cultivated for Winter flowers, owing to the yearly increasing variety of color and excellent adaptation for that purpose. They are also effective as bedding plants for garden, blooming from July until frost. 15 cents each; $1.50 per dozen; small mailing plants, $1.00 per dozen.
A. Neuner. Perfectly double, pure waxy white, a constant bloomer, and of unsurpassing beauty.
Elegans. Salmon scarlet, large and fine; a splendid color.
Humboldtii Corymbiflora. The largest white flowering sort out; the flower tubes are three inches long; very fragrant.
Leiantha. Dazzling scarlet; one of the best, and very profuse.
Maiden Blush. Bright blush pink flowers, a distinct color; an elegant acquisition.
The Bride. White, with very slight tinge of flesh; a really fine sort.
Vreelandii. Finest of the white Bouvardias; valuable for bouquets; best of all singles.
President Cleveland. A splendid novelty, extra large fiery-scarlet flowers; strong, vigorous growth.
President Garfield. A new double pink; this is a sport from the double white Bouvardia A. Neuner; novel and handsome.
Single Flavescens. Flowers of a bright canary; very desirable; sweet; reminiscent.
Bockii. New single pink; a beautiful novelty, producing single flowers in graceful clusters and producing a striking appearance.

CALADIUMS—Fancy Leaved.
We have a fine collection of first-class, distinct. They are never as large as Esculentum, but the brilliant cardinal red, pink, cream and various shades of green that are displayed in the veinings and blotches of the leaves can not be obtained in any other class of plants. 30 cents each for fine, well dried tubers.

CALADIUM ESCULENTUM.
The most striking and distinct ornamental foliage plant in cultivation; desirable for pot or tub culture, and fine for bedding out. With a plentiful supply of water, the leaves may be grown from four six feet long, and one and one-half feet in breadth. 20 cents each.

CANNA.
The Canna is a fine foliage plant, making a good bed alone, but particularly desirable as

the centre of a group of foliage plants, for which it is one of the best, growing from three to six feet. The leaves are sometimes two feet in length, of a beautiful green, some varieties tinted with Select old sorts, 10 cents each.

Ehemanni. The most distinct of all Cannas on account of its large oval soft green leaves and carmine red flowers, which are produced on long flower stems; each of the smaller branches bear about twelve flowers. The flowers are as large as a Gladiolus, and are used to advantage in bouquet making. This is one of the most striking and desirable Cannas ever introduced. 25 cents each.

Nouttoni. Is quite distinct from Ehemanni in coloring, being a rich shade of crimson scarlet. The flowers are very large, growing erect instead of drooping. The foliage is of a beautiful bluish green, growing very compact and remarkably free flowering, forming nearly so'ld masses of rich, warm coloring. The plant does not exceed six feet in height. 25 cents each.

CAPE JESAMINE.

Gardenia Florida. A Southern plant of easy cultivation, blooming profusely in Spring and early Summer; flowers pure white, double; plants very bushy; foliage dark green and glossy. Plants that will bloom, 25 and 50 cents.

Cineraria.

CINERARIA.

Hybrida. These are among the most gorgeous of our greenhouse plants: the colors range through all the shades of blue, violet crimson, pink, maroon and white. They are in bloom only until May. 10, 15, 25 and 30 cents, according to size.

CATALONIAN JESSAMINE.

Jasminum Grandiflorum. A beautiful white Jessamine, of exquisite fragrance. 15 to 50 cents each.

COCOLOBIUM.

Vesputalinous. A free-growing plant of greenhouse culture, suitable for baskets. 20 cents each.

CYCLAMEN FERSICUM.

As an ornamental greenhouse plant it is excelled by few, and its flowers as a variety in the formation of bouquets and baskets of cut flowers in Winter are valuable. 10 to 25 cents.

CACTUS.

Of these plants we have a fine collection. The Cactus family is interesting on account of the curious leafless growth of the plants

and the beauty of the flowers; the Lobster Cactus, especially, being a great favorite.

Epiphyllum Truncatum. Lobster Cactus; Winter blooming. 25 cents.

Cereus Grandiflorus. The Night Blooming Cereus. 25 cents.

CENTAUREA.

Gymnocarpa. Dusty Miller. Attains a diameter of two feet, forming a graceful round bush of silver gray, for which nothing is so well to contrast in ribbon lines with dark foliaged plants. 50 cents per dozen.

COROTONS.

The Crotons are among the finest decorative foliage plants known. The leaves of all are more or less veined and margined, sometimes entirely variegated with shades of yellow, orange and crimson. Some have long, narrow leaves, arching gracefully, in fountain-fashion; others broad and short, oak-leaved. Some recurved very much; others twisted, cork-screw like. Crotons love heat, sunshine and moisture. They make beautiful bedding plants in the heat of Summer. 50 cents each; small plants, 25 cents.

Angustifolia. Narrow leaved; red and yellow.

Aucubifolia. Foliage deep green, spotted yellow.

Aurea. Small foliage, yellow mottled on dark green ground.

Cornutum. A distinct and very compact growing variety, blotched and spotted yellow.

Discolor. Light green leaves, claret color on reverse side of leaf.

Disrae.l. The coloring of the foliage is rich and varied; shades and markings of scarlet; orange and yellow are seen on the same plant with deep green ground of the mature foliage.

Earl of Derby. A splendid Croton with leaves of the C. Disraeli form, highly colored with bright yellow, and quite distinct from every other kind.

Interruptum. This is one of the finest and most elegant of the many Crotons. It is a finely marked variety, with dark red variegation, and as its name implies.

Irregulare. Leaves about nine inches in length and most diversified in shape, scarcely two leaves resembling each other; ground dark green; mid-rib an orange yellow.

Lord Cairns. A broad leaved variety; a bright green, spotted yellow.

Mutabile. Interrupted leaves, and yellow bar.

Nobilis. The colors are crimson, yellow and green in many shades, bordered by bands of deep golden yellow.

Ovalifolio. Oval leaved, finely marked with yellow.

Pictum. Foliage dark green spotted with red and yellow.

Spiralis. Twisting foliage twelve inches long; color green and gold.

Tortolis. A remarkable interesting variety with twisted foliage.

Undulatum. Foliage metallic green, spotted crimson, pink and yellow, the edges of the leaves being beautifully undulated and wavy.

Veitchii. Leaves waxy green, marked with yellow, changing to rose, scarlet and purple.

Variegatum. Leaves dark green, striped and spotted golden yellow.

Volutum. A very distinct and beautiful form, the great peculiarity of which consists in the leaves being rolled up from the end in a volute, after the manner of the curving of a ram's horn.

Youngii. Leaves eighteen inches long, very distinct, noble and graceful habit, surface dark green, marked with creamy yellow and bright rosy red.

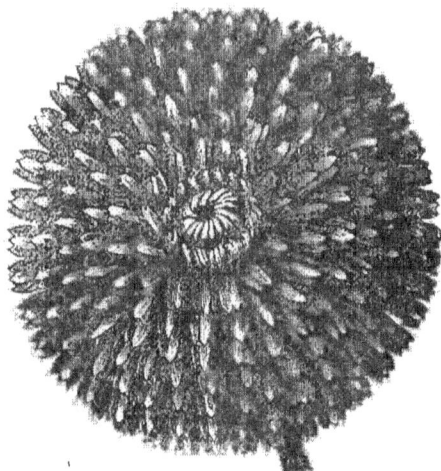

Calendula.

CALENDULA.
Showy and free-flowering hardy annuals, growing in any good garden soil, producing a fine effect in beds or mixed borders, and continuing in bloom until killed by frost. 75 cents per dozen.
Officinalis Meteor. A new splendid variety; very large and beautiful extra double striped imbricated flowers, of a deep orange on a pale yellow ground.

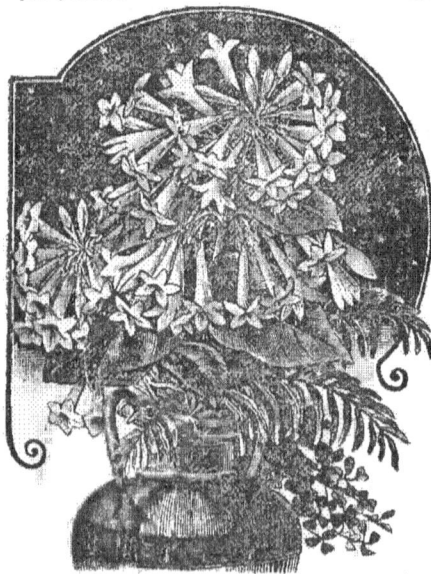

Cestrum Parqui.

CESTRUM PARQUI.
The Night-blooming Jessamine; this well known and highly prized plant, blooming nearly all the year round, is a native of Chili. An excellent garden plant, growing rapidly; foliage long and of deep green color; producing its richly fragrant flowers at every joint;

sweet only at night; it is well adapted to house and window culture. 10 cents each.

COLEUS.
The Coleus is the best and cheapest ornamental leaved plant we have for ornamental bedding, in what is sometimes called the carpet style. A few dozen of these plants will make a bed of which no one will have any cause to be ashamed. There is such an endless variety in their colors and markings that, with a little taste in planting out varieties, the most gratifying results can be obtained at a trifling cost. Plants should be set about a foot apart, so that when the size of the bed is ascertained it is easy to figure out how many plants are needed of each kind for a row. 5 cents each; 50 cents per dozen; $4.00 per 100.
Acme. Foliage broad; golden centre, veined with crimson.
Hero. Chocolate maroon, almost black.
James Barnshaw. Yellow and crimson streaked.
Kentish Fire. Centre crimson, marbled with purple.
Miss Retta Kirkpatrick. Large white centre; yellow shaded; broad green lobed margin; very large foliage.
Mrs. Wilson. Centre of leaf bright pink, border a creamy white, veined with a lighter shade of pink; light, serated margin.
Mrs. Garfield. Very bright crimson, marbled and shaded pink, with a large bar of yellow; deep green serated margin.
Verschaffeltii. Velvet crimson.
John Go do. A splendid new Coleus for bedding purposes; it is of a bright yellow color, that retains its color all through the Summer.
Golden Bedder. Pure yellow; equally as good a bedder as Verschaffeltii.
Mrs. Geddes. A crimson maroon; very bright centre; a compact grower.
Spotted Gem. Finely mottled; a free grower.
J. H. Slocomb. Good dark; very hardy.
Contrast. A dark maroon.
Yellow Bird. Good yellow.
Firebrand. Deep crimson.
Senator. Dark chocolate brown, with fiery edgings and stripes; very effective.
Hiawatha. Fine; orange yellow and crimson flamed margin. This is one of the best and most distinct.
Onward. Finely marbled and blotched with the various shades of maroon, yellow, pink, crimson, black, and white; fine.
Progress. Distinct green, covered with dots of yellow; maroon and red.
Princeps. Dark; bright crimson, with yellow margin; one of the best.
Pluto. Green ground, flaked and bordered bright carmine and chocolate base, yellowish white.

CISSUS DISCOLOR.
A well known climber, with leaves beautifully shaded dark green, purple and white, the upper surface of the leaf having a rich velvet like appearance. 15 to 30 cents.

CHRYSANTHEMUM FRUTESCENS.
This is the Paris Daisy now so fashionable and in such demand during the Winter. The flowers much resemble our common field Daisy; almost constant in bloom. 10 cents.

EUPHORBIAS.
Plants of great value for Winter blooming and making splendid pot plants; they are sure to bloom with regularity, are easily cared for, and do not suffer much from a moderate amount of neglect or abuse. 25 cents each.

CYPERUS.

Alternifolius. A grass-like plant, throwing up its stems to the height of about two feet, surmounted at the top by a cluster or whorl of leaves, diverging horizontally, giving the plant a very curious appearance; a splendid plant for the centre of baskets or wardian cases, or as a water plant. 10 cents each.

COCCOLOBA.

Platyclada. A plant of very singular and interesting growth; stem and branches growing to flat, broad points; well suited for vases and rustic work. 10 cents each.

CUPHEA.

Platycentra. (Cigar Plant.) Tube of flowers scarlet; tip white and black; very free and fine bloomer; a good basket plant; also an excellent plant for the house in the Winter. 10 cents each.

DRACÆNA—Dragon Tree.

One of the most desirable of our ornamental foliage plants for decoration, either in or out doors, as it does not appear to suffer under the dry atmosphere of rooms; in a partially shaded situation it stands remarkably well during the Summer out of doors. Its bright foliage renders it very useful for the window garden, planted as a centre-piece in a rustic stand, jardiniere, or window box, or for Summer decoration in vases, ornamental beds, etc. It thrives best in a light rich soil, composed of leaf-mould, sand, loam and thoroughly composed manure. 25, 50, 75 cents and $1.00 each.

Amabilis. Green, white and pale violet; very strong plants.

Baptisti. Green, creamy white flakes flushed with rose.

Goldeana. Irregularly banded with dark green and silver gray in alternate straight bands.

Imperialis. A strong growing variety, with large deep rose and creamy-white foliage.

Terminalis. Rich crimson foliage marked with pink and white.

Youngi. Light green changing to a copper color.

Australis. A very long, narrow, graceful foliage.

Invivisa. Long foliage; green, graceful.

Veitchi. Long foliage, brown streaked.

ECHEVERAS.

A genus of succulent plants, natives of Mexico. They are of rich appearance, and well suited for rock work.

Metallica. Large shell-like leaves, with a peculiar lilac and metallic luster; flower stems borne from about two feet high, covered with yellow and scarlet bell-shaped flowers; we know of no plant better adapted as a centre piece of small vases, baskets, etc. 25 cents.

Sanguinea. Narrow pointed leaves; color a deep red. 15 cents.

Splendens. The plant is a perfect mass of thorns, and anything but handsome, the numerous flowers, however, are bright and beautiful; they are brilliant scarlet, and borne in close clusters of six or seven; almost always in bloom; requires but little water. 25 cents.

Secunda Glauca. A dwarf sort, resembling the house Leek; glaucus green; they bloom all Summer; an excellent plant for borders. This is best known as "Hen and Chickens," or "House Leek," a most interesting plant, beautiful for edging beds or rock work; we grow them extensively. 10 cents each; $1.00 per dozen; $6.00 per 100.

EUPATORIUMS.

There is never any question about a Eupatorium blooming, and blooming well, when the season comes around; that season is the dead of Winter; and it is seldom that a Christmas box of flowers from a florist fails to contain a quantity of pure feathery white Eupatorium clusters. 10 cents each.

Augustifolium. Remains a long time in bloom; fine large white flowers.

Arboreum. Of heavier growth than the others and larger; more compact trusses; white.

Elegans. Graceful heads of the most delicate and beautiful new flowers; pure white.

Riparium. White; in bloom from January to April.

Freezia Refracta Alba.

Amazonica.

EUCHARIS.

Amazonica. The beautiful American Lily; a bulbous rooted plant, with broad Lily-like leaves and pure white flowers about four inches in diameter, borne in heads of four or five, and deliciously fragrant. Give them an abundance of water when growing and blooming. Fine bulbs, 50 cents.

FREEZIA REFRACTA ALBA.

A bulbous rooted plant of easiest cultivation; the flower is pure white, spotted with lemon yellow; in shape like a miniature Gladiolus, only more extended and deliciously sweet; will bloom best planted out during Summer. 10 cents.

Ctsse. Louise Erclody.

BEGONIA REX CTSS'. LOUISE ERC! ODY.

This is the Begonia of all Begonias. Its striking peculiarity, which distinguishes it from all Begonias, consists in the two lobes not growing side by side, but one winds itself in a spiral way repeatedly over itself. 35 cents each.

FEVERFEW.

Little Gem. The finest double white yet raised, blooming very freely and being more dwarf, with larger and more double flowers than the old variety; a first-class pant, that everyone should have. 10 cents.

Double White. Very free blooming, double, Daisy-like flower; very useful for Summer bouquets.

FICUS.

Elastica. India Rubber Tree One of the best plants for table or parlor decoration; its thick leathery leaves enable it to stand excessive heat and dryness, while its deep glossy green color always presents a cheerful aspect. The plants we offer are in fine order and are of a size to be useful immediately. 75 cents to $1.50 each.

Auricaria Excelsa. A beautiful evergreen tree of handsome uniformity of growth, the branches produced at right angles all t e way up the main stem; must be seen to be appreciated; very scarce. Small plants, $1.00 each; nice strong plants, $8.00 each

Auricaria Imbricata. Known as the "Monkey Puzzler," being covered with sharp t orns. It is said it is the only tree the monkey can't climb Small plants, $1.00 each; large plants, $5.00 each.

FERNS.

These very beautiful plants are now very generally cultivated; their great diversity and gracefulness of foliage make them much valued as plants for vases, baskets, or rock work, or as specimen plants for parlor and conservatory. 15 cents.

FORGET-ME-NOT.

Myosotis Palustris. Requires no description. Its clustered flowers of beautiful blue having had a place in romance and literature since romance and literature began; the plants need a moist, somewhat shaded location. 10 cents each.

JASIMINUM.

Grandiflorum. Catalonian Jesamine. A valuable Winter-flowering plant, blooming without intermission from October to May; the flowers are pure white, and most deliciously fragrant. 15, 25 and 50 cents each.

Grand Duke Flowers are double; white like miniature Roses; deliciously fragrant. 75 cents each.

Gladioli.

GLADIOLI.

Among bulbous flowers the Gladiolus deserves first place in popular favor Our collection is very fine, a good assortment of colors, red, pink, striped and many shades of light colors. By express, 75 cents per dozen; by mail, $1.00 per dozen.

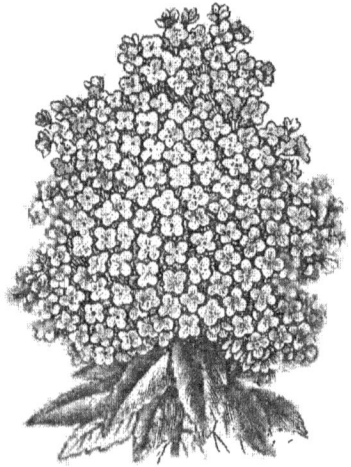

Hydrangea.

HYDRANGEAS.

Hortensia. The well known garden variety; has immense heads of pink flowers, which hang on for months. 15 cents.

Otaksa. Heads large flowers a bright rosy pink, contrasting beautifully with other sorts; of low bushy growth. 10 cents.

Thomas Hogg. Immense truss of flowers, at first tinged with green, then turning pure white, and remaining so a long time. 15 cents.

GLOXINIA.

GLOXINIA.

Gloxinias are among the handsomest of our Summer-blooming greenhouse plants. Bulbs should be started in the Spring, in a warm place. They require partial shade and a liberal supply of water when growing. After blooming, water should be withheld, and the bulbs remain dry during the Winter. 50 cents each; small plants, 15 cents each.

Hibiscus.

HIBISCUS.

A beautiful class of greenhouse shrubs, with handsome glossy foliage, and large, showy flowers, often measuring four inches in diameter; they succeed admirably bedded out during the Summer. 15 cents each.

Brilliantissima. Single flowers, of the richest crimson scarlet; dark crimson at the base of petals; very large and showy.

Denisonii Rosea. Large, single flowers, a clear transparent rose.

Grandiflora. Enormous rosy crimson, single flowers, which are produced in the greatest abundance.

Kermesinus. Enormous, very double, rich carmine crimson.

Lutea. Yellow flowering; very pretty.

Minratus Semi-Plenus. An immense and semi-double flower, dark vermilion scarlet.

Zobrinus. Outer petals scarlet, edged with yellow; variegated with yellow and scarlet.

Magnificus. Very large flower and of perfect form; color deep magenta, edge of petals touched with brown.

Schisopetalus. A very curiously formed flower pendant, the petals in a whorl; an orange red.

Dracæna Ind.visa. (See page 54).

HOYA—Wax Plant.

Carnosa. Star-shaped, waxy flowers, in clusters; beautiful, thick, glossy, evergreen leaves; excellent for house decoration, as it stands the dry heat of a sitting room with impunity. 25 cents each.

HELIOTROPE.

A great favorite on account of the delicate fragrance of its flowers; a constant bloomer when planted out in a sunny, warm place, the colors varying from nearly white to dark purple. By express, our selection, 25 for $1.00; by mail, 20 for $1.00. Purchaser's selection, 10 cents each; 75 cents per dozen.

Albert Delaux. A French novelty of great beauty; bright golden yellow foliage, and marked with delicate green, the deep lavender color of the flower contrasting admirably with the ever varying foliage.

Chieftain. Rich shade of violet; best Winter bloomer.

Chatoyant. A new shade, deep rosy-violet tint, with clear white eye.

Forget-Me-Not. Large flowers, fully one-half larger than the old variety; color a light lavender, large, finely formed flowers.

Jersey Beauty. The finest blue variety; best for pot culture; dwarf.

King of Night. Dark royal purple, almost a black, dotted in the centre with a distinct white eye.

Louise Delaux. Beautiful rose color, lightly shaded violet; plant erect, neat in habit, and very floriferous.

Mrs. David Wood. The semi-double Heliotrope. We give the grower's description: "Flowers in large heads; a fragrant, early and constant bloomer; light blue."

President Garfield. A gem of the first water; fine deep blue, very floriferous.

White Lady. A strong growing, free branching plant, very profuse in bloom; flowers large and of the purest white.

Queen of Violets. Very dark purple.

KLENIA RETICULATA.

A very pretty succulent plant, with glaucous fleshy leaves. 15 cents each.

LANTANAS.

Plants much used for bedding and pot culture; they are strong growing and constant bloomers. 10 cents each; $1.00 per dozen.

Antantiaca. Beautiful orange.

Jacob Schultz. Flowers red, changing to crimson.

Purpurea. Good purple.

Rosa Mundi. White and rose.

IMPATIENS.
Sultani. A new plant of the same order as the well known Balsams, but differing widely from them in the habit of blooming; the flowers are borne in clusters or masses around the head of the plant, and are single, beautifully formed, and colored a carmine magenta, at times so dark as to become almost purple. 15 cents each.

LIBONIAS.
Floribunda. Long flowers, shaded from orange scarlet at the base to deep yellow at the mouth; they bloom with great profusion during Winter. 10 cents each.
Penrhosiensis. Another Winter blooming plant of neat and pretty habit; flowers of a bright rich crimson, changing to a fiery red. 10 cents each.

LYCOPODIUM.
Denticulatum. Chinese Moss. This is the most popular of the creeping Mosses, creeping in dense masses over the soil; loves shade and moisture like all the rest. 15 cents.

NASTURTIUM.
Empress of India. The plant is of a very dwarf habit, with dark tinted foliage, while the flowers are of the most brilliant crimson color, so freely produced that no other annual in cultivation can approach it in effectiveness; so highly was this Nasturtium considered, that the Royal Horticultural Society of London awarded it a first-class certificate, an award never given except in novelties of undoubted merit. 10 cents.

OXALIS.
These plants are of the easiest possible culture, and are fine for baskets, vases, etc.
Lutea. Large clear yellow flowers, in great profusion. 15 cents.
Rubra. Flowers bright red.
White. Color white; these varieties flower in the greatest profusion, Winter and Summer. 10 cents.

OLEANDER.
Double Pink. The oldest and finest of all varieties in cultivation; flowers double and rose colored. 20 cents each.
Lilian Henderson. A new double, and one of the best yet introduced. 50 cents each.

PRIMULA OBCONICA.
This is undoubtedly one of the most useful flowering plants grown; the seedlings will begin to bloom in May or June and continue to bloom during the whole year. The flowers are of a soft lilac shade and very charming. It is one of the most useful Primulas for pot culture, and also succeeds well in the open border during the Summer months. 20 cents each; $2.00 per dozen.

MUSA ENSETE.
The noblest of all plants is this great Abyssinian Banana. The fruit of this variety is not edible, but the leaves are magnificent, long, broad and of a beautiful green, with a broad crimson midrib. The plant grows luxuriantly from eight to twelve feet high. During the hot Summer, when planted out, it grows rapidly and attains gigantic proportions, producing a tropical effect on the lawn, terrace or flower garden. It can be stored in a light cellar or cool greenhouse during the Winter, with a covering of soil, or planted in a tub, watered sparingly. We offer a fine lot of these plants, at $1.00, $1.50, $2.00 and $3.00 each; a few extra strong plants, $5.00 each.

MAHERNIA ODORAMA.
A profuse Winter blooming plant, with golden yellow flowers, that emit a strong honeyed fragrance. 10 cents each.

MARANTA.
Zebrina. An ornamental leaved plant of very great beauty; leaves large, with bands of dark velvety green; fine for ferneries. 50 cents each.

PETUNIAS—Double.
Few plants have been so much improved as the Petunias. The double flowers are of much greater size than the largest of the singles, and are very richly colored. They flower freely, and continue often even after hard frost. They make splendid pot plants for early Spring blooming. 15 cents.

POINSETTIA PULCHERRIMA.
A new double Poinsettia; a very brilliant scarlet, tinted with orange color; a dazzling color; the head grows on a specimen plant fourteen inches in diameter by ten inches in depth, giving it the appearance of a cone of fire. 25 cents each.

PANSIES.
This lovely flower, a favorite with every one, is too well known to need any description. Nothing can be more effective, whether grown in beds, ribbons, groups, or interspersed among other plants in the border. It is also admirably adapted for pot culture for the decoration of the conservatory during the Winter and Spring months. The plants offered are from the very finest strains of seed, and will, we are sure, give entire satisfaction. Pansies seem to have well founded claims to become the American national flower. First, they are the favorite flower of the first lady in the land, and we are quite certain, with the ladies in general. 20 for $1.00 by express, 16 for $1.00 by mail, $4.00 per 100.
I know they can't talk,
  Though they sometimes look like they wink,
But I tell you this for a secret,
  I really believe they think.

PILEA.
Arborea. The Artillery Plant. A pretty little plant of drooping habit, resembling the Fern; it is a fine basket plant. 15 cents.

PLUMBAGO.
The Plumbagos are desirable on account of their beautiful shades of blue, a color by no means too common among our flowering plants.
Capensis. Very bright plants, producing large heads of light blue flowers. 15 cents each.

PRIMROSE—Chinese.
Few house plants afford more genuine satisfaction than this. It requires to be keep cool, a north window suiting it best. Primroses are at present all in bloom. 20 cents each, $2.00 per dozen.
  A Primrose by the river's brim,
  A yellow Primrose 'twas to him,
  And it was nothing more.

RUSSELIA JUNCEA.
Has long, very graceful, rush-like foliage, the drooping tips of which bear tubular, light scarlet blossoms in showers; there is nothing so beautiful for large vases; a handsome house plant. 25 cents.

STEVIA.
While Winter blooming plants of great value; in style of growth and free flowering qualities resembling Eupatoriums, although botanically distinct, and requiring the same treatment. 15 cents each.

STREPTOSOLEN JAMESONI.
Resembles in growth the Brownlias; the flowers are lobed, nearly one inch in diameter, opening bright orange and passing to rich, deep cinnabar red; it commences to flower early in March, continuing through June and July. 15 cents.

SALVIA—Flowering Sage.
This plant is indispensable in the garden in Autumn. They may be planted in masses or scattered among the shrubbery; in either way their gorgeous effect is well displayed. 10 cents each, except where noted; $1.00 per doz. Our selection, 20 for $1.00.
Mrs. Edward Mitchell. It is a distinct crimson purple.
Mrs. Stevens. Dark maroon.

Purpurea. Dark purple.

Patens. This is the most exquisite blue of any flower we have; nothing new, but an old popular favorite. 25 cents.

Ratilans. Apple scented; produces very neat spikes of magenta colored flowers; graceful foliage, with an agreeable apple fragrance.

Splendens. Flower spikes of most brilliant scarlet.

Splendens Alba. White flowered variety of Splendeus.

TRADESCANTIA.

Zebrina. Wandering Jew. Leaves striped, a silvery white. $1.00 per dozen.

SMILAX.

A climbing plant, unsurpassed in the graceful beauty of its foliage; its peculiar wavy formation renders it one of the most valuable plants for bouquets, wreaths, festoons and decorations. 15 cents each.

TUBEROSE.

Pearl. New double. Flowers of large size, imbrieuted like a Rose, dwarf habit, growing only from eighteen inches to two feet high. 10 cents; 50 cents per dozen; $3.00 per 100. By express, 30 for $1.00.

VIOLETS.

It is one of the leading florists' flowers for bouquets and cut flowers. All the varieties should have a slight protection of leaves during the Winter. A better plan to insure early Spring flowers is, to plant in cold frames in the Fall. They thrive best in a shady situation, in rich, deep soil. 10 cents each.

Blue Neapolitan. Double light lavendar blue; very profuse bloomer.

Marie Louise. Double, darker than the above, and larger in size.

Czar. Single, rich bluish purple; large.

Schœnbrun. Single, dark blue; profuse.

Single White. White blooming.

Victoria Regina. The largest of the single flowing varieties; dark purple.

Swanley White New double white, a pure white violet, which is never tinged with any other shade under any other condition. Flowers are as large as that of Marie Louise.

VINCA—Periwinkle.

Best blooming plant for bedding out, being constantly in bloom from June until frost, bearing the hot sun and frequent drouth well; excellent for the South. We have a good stock. 10 cents each; 50 cents per dozen; $1.00 per 100.

Alba. Pure white; hundreds of flowers on one plant

Rosa Alba. Pure white; dark rose eye.

Rosea. Dark rose pink.

CLIMBERS.

ARISTOLOCHIA SIPHO.—Dutchman's Pipe.

Very large leaves and brownish flowers of a very singular shape, resembling a pipe; it is a vigorous and rapid growing climber, attaining a height of twenty feet. 25 cents each.

AKEBIA QUINATA.

A climbing plant from Japan, with beautiful nut foliage, having large clusters of chocolate colored flowers, which are very fragrant. Attains the height of twenty feet. 25 cents each.

IMPOMEA NOCTIFLORA.—The Evening Glory, or Moon Flower.

There are few plants we have seen sent out that have been so satisfactory as this; hundreds to whom we have sent it have written to us about the satisfaction it has given. One lady says that it was trained on strings to a balcony twenty-five feet high and forty

feet wide, and that from August to November it was covered nightly with its white moon-like flowers from five to six inches in diameter; it has also a rich, Jessamine-like odor at night. 20 cents each.

ALLAMANDAS.

The Allamandas are beautiful, evergreen climbers, with rich, glossy foliage, and deep yellow flowers, which are very large and showy. It would be difficult to exaggerate the beauty of the Allamandas or their real, permanent value. 50 cents each.

WISTARIA SINENSIS.

One of the most hardy climbing plants, and when once established, of rapid growth, covering the entire side of a house in a few years, presenting a magnificent appearance when in full bloom, with its thousands of rich clusters in pendulus racemes of delicate violet blue blossoms, richly perfumed. 50 cents.

AMPELOPSIS.

Quinquefolia. A rapid grower, attaching itself to brick or stone walls or trees; beautiful green foliage in Summer, turning to rich crimson in Autumn. 25 cents.

Veitchii. A miniature variety of Virginia Creeper, which clings to any building, and produces in the greatest profusion dense foliage of glossy pale green, shaded with purple, and which turns brilliantly red in Autumn; of exceedingly rapid growth, and requires no nailing; perfectly hardy. 25 cents each.

CLERODENDRON

Balfouri. A very handsome greenhouse climber, with large clusters of crimson-scarlet flowers, each flower encased in a bag-like calyx of pure white. 25 cents.

PASSIFLORA.—Passion Flower.

Will bloom a long time in the house if grown in a large pot or tub and removed before frost. 50 cents each.

Decaisneana. Flowers large, of a deep, rich purple, with lively markings; plants must be large before they bloom.

Piordtii. Fine rapid grower; very free bloomer; color purple, very large and beautiful.

Quadrangularis Folia Variegata. This is a magnificent novelty. The foliage is beautiful in itself, deep olive green, blotched and dotted with rich golden yellow. The flowers are very large and sweet scented; color purple inside of petals, light green on the outside; the center of the flower is of many colors

CISSUS DISCOLOR.

A well-known climber, with leaves beautifully shaded dark green, purple and white, the upper surface of the leaf having a rich, velvety-like appearance. 15 to 30 cents each.

COBÆA.

Scandens. A magnificent climber, with large, bell-shaped flowers and elegant leaves and tendrils; it is of rapid growth, and consequently eminently adapted during the Summer for warm situations, where it will produce an abundance of its elegant purple flowers. 20 cents each.

RHNCOSPERMUM.

Jasminoides. A greenhouse climber, with white Jessamine-like flowers, which are produced in great clusters in the Spring months, and have a delicious fragrance. 25 cents.

Select Hardy Evergreen Trees.

JUNIPERS.

Irish. Erect and formal in its habit; much used in cemeteries. Three to four feet, $1.00 each. We have a nice lot of young Irish Junipers and Retinosporas about 8 to 10

Inches high, well rooted, at 15 cents each; these can be sent by mail if necessary.

Juniper Dwarf. 10 cents each.

Hemlock. A remarkably graceful and beautiful tree, with drooping branches and delicate dark foliage of the Yew. 50 cents each.

Arbor Vitæ, Golden. A beautiful variety of Chinese, compact and globular in form; color a lively yellowish green. 50 cents.

Arbor Vitæ, Semper Aurea. A variety of the Aurea of dwarf habit, but free growth, retaining its golden tint all the year round. 50 to 75 cents.

Arbor Vitæ, American. This plant is, all things considered, the finest Evergreen. 25 to 50 cents.

Arbor Vitæ, Tom Thumb. A very small, compact little Evergreen; a beautiful ornament for a small yard or cemetery lot. 50 to 75 cents.

Arbor Vitæ, Hoveyi. A small tree, globular in form; foliage light green, with a golden tinge 50 to 75 cents.

Arbor Vitæ, Pumila. A little dwarf; very fine both in color and form. 50 to 75 cents.

MAHONIA AQUIFOLIA—Holly-leaved. Evergreens with bright shiny leaves and showy bunches of yellow flowers in the early Spring. 25 cents.

MAGNOLIA.
Grandiflora. The true Southern Magnolia; of great beauty; too well known to need description. Nice pot plants, sure to grow, about 18 inches high, 75 cents. This size is much safer to plant than the larger sizes.

BOX.
Dwarf. Fine for edging. 10 cents each; $4.00 per 100.

SPRUCE.
Norway. A lofty elegant tree of perfect pyramidal habit; very popular, should be largely planted. One of the best Evergreens. 50 cents.

Arbor Vitæ, Ericoides. Very pretty dense little shrub of the Tom Thumb type. 50 to 75 cents each.

Arbor Vitæ, Pyramidalis. An exceedingly beautiful, bright variety, resembling the Irish Juniper in form. 50 to 75 cents each.

Retinospora, Plumosa. An exceedingly handsome Evergreen from Japan, with feathery, light green foliage. 75 cents each.

Retinospora, Plumosa Aurea. Like the preceding, a plant of great beauty, soft, plume-like foliage. $1.00 each.

Yew, Irish. Upright in growth, with dense foliage of a dark sombre hue; valuable for cemeteries or small yards. $1.00 each; strong young plants, 50 cents each.

SIBERIAN ARBORVITÆ.
The best Arborvitæ for this country. Exceedingly hardy, keeping its color well in Winter. 25 and 50 cents each.

Hardy Herbaceous Shrubs, Etc.

DEUTZIA GRACILIS.
Graceful white blooms, produced all the Spring in large quantities; dwarf and bushy. 25 cents each.

LYCHIUS CALCEODONICA.
A beautiful Summer-flowering plant, entirely hardy; flowers in June. 10 cents each.

CAMPANULA CARPATICA.
The old Canterbury bell; a beautiful cup-shaped garden flower and a great favorite everywhere. 10 cents.

CALYCANTHUS FLORIDUS.
This is the "Shrub" of all gardens, with sweet-scented flowers in early May. 50 cents.

ERIANTHUS RAVENNÆ.—Ravenna Grass.
Perfectly hardy; the foliage forms graceful clumps three to four feet high, above which arise numerous spikes five or six feet, bearing plumy flowers. 50 cents.

AZALEA AMERICANA.
Hardy Azaleas; are deciduous; flowers in May; light straw-colored blossoms, very beautiful. 50 cents each.

IRIS SUSIANA.—The Mourning Bride.
The groundwork of the flower is a silvery gray, shaded and lined with very dark chocolate and black. 25 cents each.

IXIAS.
These are amongst the most graceful and beautiful of half-hardy bulbs. 25 cents each.

HOLLYHOCKS.
Superb Double Kinds. The Hollyhock is becoming a very popular Summer-flowering plant, and when planted in rich soil and sunny position it is a very impressive and stately plant. We offer strong, one-year old plants at $1.00 per dozen. Nice young plants that will bloom this year, 50 cents per dozen.

EULALIA.
Japonica Zebriana. Unlike other variegated plants, this has its striping or marking across the leaf instead of longitudinally; the extended flower spike resembles the ostrich plume, and will last for years. 25 cents.

ASTILBE JAPONICA.
Incomparably the most beautiful of hardy herbaceous plants, growing about two feet high, in compact shape, with handsome foliage, from above which rise its panicles of small, feathery, white blossoms. 25 cents each.

ANEMONE.—Wind Flower.
A very pleasing hardy perennial, bulbous-rooted plant; easily grown from seed; producing very large flowers early in the Spring, in a sunny situation. 10 cents.

DIANTHUS.—Pinks.
A magnificent genus, embracing some of the most popular flowers in cultivation. 10 cents each.

IRIS.—Fleur-de-Lis
The Iris is a very extensive and beautiful family, commonly known as the Flowering Flag. 25 cents each.

WIEGELIAS.
Beautiful shrubs that bloom in June and July. The flowers are produced in so great profusion as to almost hide the foliage. 25 cents.

IRIS KÆMPFERII.
They are very hardy, and of most distinct and showy colors, flowering for a period of five to seven weeks. 25 cents.

PÆONIAS.
Pæonias, like other meritorious plants, have always admirers. 30 cents.

VIBURNUM PLICATUM.—Japanese Snowball.
A beautiful shrub of moderate upright growth, with crinkled or plicated rich green leaves. The flowers are white, and larger and more solid than those of the common Snowball. 25 and 50 cents.

PHILADELPHUS.—Mock Orange.
Coronarius. A medium-sized shrub, bearing an abundance of white, sweet-scented flowers; last of May. 25 cents.

DEUTZIA.
Crenata. Height, two to three feet; regular and compact form; very bushy; flower pure white; blooms profusely; very hardy. 25 cents.

CRAPE MYRTLE.
Pink. Fringed pink blossoms.
Crimson. Deep crimson. 10 cents.

HYDRANGEA PANICULATA GRANDIFLORA.
One of the finest hardy shrubs in cultivation; the flowers are formed in large white panticles or trusses, nine inches to one foot in length. 25 to 50 cents.

SPIRÆA.
Reovosii Flora Picna. A charming shrub with narrow, pointed leaves, and large round clusters of double white flowers. 25 cents.

TAMARIX CALLICA.
The pink flowers of the Tamarisk, borne all along its slender branches, and its delicate feathery foliage give it a character no other shrub possesses. 50 cents.

PHLOX.
Our collection embraces the best of the old varieties and the new French ones of recent introduction, which are very fine, distinct, pure colors, many of them beautifully shaded and marked with distinct, clear, light eyes. 15 cents. $1.50 per dozen.

Grapes, Raspberries, Etc.

GRAPES.
Concord. Black; best for general cultivation. Two years, 15 cents each.
Ives' Seedling. Dark purple. Two years, 15 cents each.
Moore's Early. Large black, excellent. Two years. 25 cents each.
Pocklington. Golden yellow. Two years. 30 cents each.
Hartford Prolific. Black; fine and early. Two years. 15 cents.
Prentiss. Greenish white. Two years. 30 cents.

RASPBERRIES.
Turner. A very hardy kind, which character makes it the favorite in the South.
Gregg. One of the best and largest.
Hansel. One of the earliest; bright scarlet.
Cutbarth. Rich and luscious; crimson.
Price, 50 cents per dozen; $2.50 per 100

GOOSEBERRIES.
Downing. Very large, handsome pale green, and of splendid quality for both cooking and table use; bush a vigorous grower, and usually free from mildew. 20 cents; $2.00 per dozen.
Houghton Seedling. Small to medium; pale red, roundish oval, sweet, tender, and very good; plants spreading, and shoots slender; enormously productive. 15 cents; $1.50 per dozen.

CURRANTS.
Large two year old plants, 15 cents; $1.50 per dozen.
Red Dutch. Old reliable sort.
White Grape. The best white.
Black Naples. An old variety.

BLACKBERRIES.
Early Harvest. Very early.
Kittatiny. Large berry.
Snyder. Hardiest of all. 50 cents per dozen; $2.50 per 100.

STRAWBERRIES.
We grow the following varieties in quantity at 75 cents per 100, $5.00 per 1,000; Charles Downing, Kentucky, Cumberland Triumph, Sharpless, May King, Wilson's Albany, Jersey Queen. We have found the following two varieties to be especially suited to this climate and highly recommend them. $1.00 per 100; $7.00 per 1,000:
The "Henderson." This valuable seedling was named by the originator in honor of Peter Henderson. It is doubtful if there is another Strawberry in cultivation having such a combination of good qualities as the Henderson. The fruit is of the largest size, early, and immensely productive, but its excelling merit is its exquisite flavor.
Hoffman's Scedling. This is a variety raised in North Carolina, and it is particularly adapted to the South. It is early, and stands the dry Summers better than any other variety we grow. We can recommend it highly for its earliness and productiveness.
Strawberry plants can only be sent by express. At this rate, if wanted by mail, add 10 cents per 25, or 30 cents per 100 for postage.

Vegetable Plants.

ASPARAGUS.
The preparation of the Asparagus-bed should be made with care, from the fact that it is a permanent crop which ought to yield well for twenty five years. The ground must be thoroughly drained; light sandy loam is preferable. Work in about six inches of manure, two feet deep, as the roots of the plant will reach that depth in a few years. The crowns of the plants should be placed at least three and a half inches below the surface. The surface of the bed should have a top-dressing of three-fourths inches of rough stable manure every fall. Salt is also a good manure. Two-year old roots, $1.00 per 100; $6.00 per 1,000.

RHUBARB, OR PIE PLANT.
This deserves to be ranked among the best and earliest fruits in the garden. It affords the earliest material for pies and tarts, continues long in use and is valuable for canning. Make the border very rich and deep. $1.50 per dozen.

TOMATO PLANTS.
We grow all the newest and best Mikado Advance, Thoburns, New Jersey, Volunteer, Dwarf Champion and many others. We grow them in small pots and they can be shipped with the greatest safety, and not disturbing the roots. By Express 50 cents per dozen; $4.00 per hundred. Ready after February 1st.

EGG.
25 cents per dozen.

PEPPER.
25 cents per dozen.

SWEET POTATO.
30 cents per 100; $2.50 per 1,000.

CABBAGE.
We have a handsome lot of about 100,000 Cabbage plants, wintered in cold frames, of following varieties: Landreth's Earliest, Winning Star, Early Flat Dutch, Early Drumhead, Select Jersey, Wakefield and others. Price per 100 50 cents; $1.00 per 1,000; in lots of more than 1,000 a special rate will be given. The plants are fine and can be shipped any time after January 1st. Young plants from seed bed after April 1st. $2.00 per 1,000.

Gold Fish.

In a large pool in one of our greenhouses devoted to the culture of tropical acquatic plants, we have succeeded in raising a fine lot of handsome gold fish. There is nothing more attractive in a room, and there is but little trouble in keeping them. Change the water two or three times a week, river or cistern water will do, and clean the globe once a week. Feed the fish wafer crackers, only a little at a time. They can be sent any distance by express in tin cans at buyer's risk. Price for small fish just commencing to color, 25 cents each. Large finely colored fish, 50 cents each. Cans for shipping fish, 15 cents each; as many as two dozen can be sent in one can.

www.ingramcontent.com/pod-product-compliance
Lightning Source LLC
Chambersburg PA
CBHW021537270326
41930CB00008B/1298